ROUTLEDGE LIBRARY EDITIONS: FREE WILL AND DETERMINISM

Volume 1

CAUSATION, FREEDOM AND DETERMINISM

CAUSATION, FREEDOM AND DETERMINISM

An Attempt to Solve the Causal Problem Through a Study of its Origins in Seventeenth-Century Philosophy

MORTIMER TAUBE

LONDON AND NEW YORK

First published in 1936 by George Allen & Unwin Ltd

This edition first published in 2017
by Routledge
2 Park Square, Milton Park, Abingdon, Oxon OX14 4RN

and by Routledge
711 Third Avenue, New York, NY 10017

Routledge is an imprint of the Taylor & Francis Group, an informa business

© 1936 George Allen & Unwin Ltd

All rights reserved. No part of this book may be reprinted or reproduced or utilised in any form or by any electronic, mechanical, or other means, now known or hereafter invented, including photocopying and recording, or in any information storage or retrieval system, without permission in writing from the publishers.

Trademark notice: Product or corporate names may be trademarks or registered trademarks, and are used only for identification and explanation without intent to infringe.

British Library Cataloguing in Publication Data
A catalogue record for this book is available from the British Library

ISBN: 978-1-138-63228-8 (Set)
ISBN: 978-1-315-20086-6 (Set) (ebk)
ISBN: 978-1-138-63493-0 (Volume 1) (hbk)
ISBN: 978-1-138-63508-1 (Volume 1) (pbk)
ISBN: 978-1-315-20660-8 (Volume 1) (ebk)

Publisher's Note
The publisher has gone to great lengths to ensure the quality of this reprint but points out that some imperfections in the original copies may be apparent.

Disclaimer
The publisher has made every effort to trace copyright holders and would welcome correspondence from those they have been unable to trace.

CAUSATION, FREEDOM AND DETERMINISM

AN ATTEMPT TO SOLVE THE CAUSAL PROBLEM THROUGH
A STUDY OF ITS ORIGINS IN SEVENTEENTH-
CENTURY PHILOSOPHY

by

MORTIMER TAUBE, Ph.D.

LONDON
GEORGE ALLEN & UNWIN LTD
MUSEUM STREET

FIRST PUBLISHED IN 1936

All rights reserved
PRINTED IN GREAT BRITAIN BY
UNWIN BROTHERS LTD., WOKING

TO
MY FATHER AND MOTHER

PREFACE

As indicated in the title, this essay falls roughly into two divisions: (1) a re-examination of historical materials, and (2) a positive theory of causation suggested by the results of this re-examination. The historical study discloses an ambiguity in the meanings of causation and determinism; it discloses also that this ambiguity is transferred to the meaning of freedom. On the whole, the thinkers of the seventeenth century had a clear understanding of the meanings of these concepts and of their relations to one another. Hume and Kant, however, failed to understand these relations, and thus perpetuated certain confusions which have made discussions of causation a most unsatisfactory portion of contemporary philosophic inquiry.

The central confusion consists in a failure to distinguish propositions concerning the order of nature and propositions describing an observed relation between two particulars. The latter may have intuitive sanction secured through the medium of direct experience, whereas the former must always be of a highly speculative and problematic nature. Propositions which assert universal determinism or the ubiquity of the "law of causation" are propositions about the order of nature; propositions about the causal relation should be descriptions of immediate matter of fact. This distinction holds *mutatis mutandis* between the concepts of determinism and freedom. Since the latter has intuitive sanction, the opposition between freedom and universal determinism is not an opposition between contradictory intuitions, but an opposition between a disclosure of immediate experience and highly abstract speculative considerations. It follows that the evidence for freedom should lead to a reformulation of our conclusions concerning the order of nature. The opposite procedure, i.e. refusing credence to the intuition of freedom, is tantamount to denying the existence of an observed black swan because we believe the general proposition that all swans are white.

That the correct procedure has not been followed seems to me to be the result of supposing that freedom is *opposed* to causation. If this were the case, we should have contrasting intuitions. The main purpose of the historical portions of this essay has been to show that for certain representative seventeenth-century philosophers the intuition of causal action is identical with the intuition of freedom. Consequently, we have little historical justification for borrowing the intuitive sanction of causation to aid the cause of determinism against freedom. In a recent work which appeared too late for consideration in the body of this work there is an excellent example of the confusions which are generated by the failure to understand this point. "We believe that everything which happens is due to something else which caused it to happen. This is the belief in the Law of Causation. We also believe that when we decide to do one thing rather than another, then we are free to do otherwise. For example, you were free to get up five minutes earlier this morning. This is the belief in Free-will. Now by the law of causation your decision to act as you did was due to something which happened before, that is, was caused and determined by what had gone before. But, if this is so, how can we say that you were free to act otherwise?"[1] Now it is obvious that the belief in freedom, if it has any basis at all, has its basis in the direct consciousness or feeling of a power to act in one way or another, i.e. it has intuitive sanction or none at all. But no one has ever directly experienced the "Law of Causation" or intuited every event and all their causes. Hence the beliefs are not of the same *type*, and the verdict of any empirical philosophy worthy of the name should be decisive in dismissing the "Law of Causation" as a false generalization. There is here no genuine antinomy, but only a failure to distinguish between a perception of matter of fact (the perception of freedom or causal efficacy) and a belief in a general proposition (the "Law of Causation").

With these conclusions as premises, I have endeavoured to show that the attempt to reduce the causal relation to the relation of succession results from the desire to explain matter-of-fact relations consistently with a dogmatic determinism. To assert the truth of absolute determinism is to deny the possibility of freedom or causal action. If such dogmatism is abandoned—and it should be since it is little more than a theological relic masquerading as a pronouncement of science—it then becomes possible to construct a theory of causation based directly upon the empirical fact of power. The elaboration of such a theory comprises the second part of this essay.

The incompleteness of some of the historical discussion I hope some day to remedy in another work on the doctrines of substance in the seventeenth century. I would refer anyone who found the absence of such material a barrier to understanding to the

[1] John Wisdom, *Problems of Mind and Matter*, 110.

works of Whitehead, especially the historical chapters in *Process and Reality.* How much I owe to Whitehead will be obvious.

I wish to acknowledge the help I received from my wife, who read and criticized the first draft of this work and helped to prepare the final version.

CONTENTS

CHAPTER		PAGE
	Preface	7
I.	PRELIMINARY DEFINITIONS	13
II.	THE ARGUMENTS FOR DETERMINISM IN SEVENTEENTH-CENTURY PHILOSOPHY	39
III.	SCIENCE AND DETERMINISM	102
IV.	HUME'S SCEPTICISM IN ITS RELATION TO CAUSATION AND DETERMINISM	130
V.	THE PERCEPTION OF CAUSAL EFFICACY	155
VI.	MATTER, CAUSATION, AND DETERMINISM	192
VII.	FREEDOM AND UNIFORMITY	222
	Appendix	251
	Bibliography	257
	Index	261

CAUSATION, FREEDOM AND DETERMINISM

CHAPTER I

PRELIMINARY DEFINITIONS

THOSE who debate the meanings or truth of propositions which assert that finite existents are free, or are determined, or causally influence other finite existents, are usually agreed on one point: and that is that many of the debates are concerned solely with the use of language. Locke,[1] Leibniz,[2] Hume,[3] and others bring this charge against their opponents. They imply that the whole question arises from a muddle in language, and that accurate definition would solve the entire problem. But the truth of propositions is a question of fact and not of meaning, and cannot be decided even in terms of the most accurate definition. On the other hand, definition, or a statement of the meaning of the terms employed, decides the relation of the truth and falsity of any one of these propositions to the others. It is this question of relations which led the philosophers we are to consider to experiment with definition.

In terms of the definitions current in the seventeenth century the propositions "finite existents are free" and "finite existents are determined" could not both be true. Hence philosophers who wished to assert

[1] J. Locke, *An Essay on the Human Understanding*, 171.
[2] G. W. von Leibniz, *Correspondence with Clarke*, 161.
[3] D. Hume, *A Treatise of Human Nature*, II, 120, 122.

both propositions were led to attempt definitions of freedom and of determinism that would make the truth of both propositions compatible. The usual procedure was to qualify either the conventional meaning of freedom or the conventional meaning of determinism. The presence of the third proposition further complicated the question. Has the truth or falsity of the proposition "finite existents causally influence other finite existents" any relation either to the proposition which asserts freedom, or to the proposition which asserts determinism? We shall find that, in spite of a certain ambiguity in the notion of causal efficacy, there was fairly general agreement that the propositions asserting causal influence and the proposition asserting determinism could not both be true. The fact of general agreement on this point was possible, since the religious questions which intruded themselves into any discussion of freedom were happily lacking. The proposition "finite existents are determined" had religious and theological sanction, whereas the proposition "finite existents exert causal influence" *prima facie* did not. Hence there was no attempt to explain away their incompatibility. However, except in the cases of Leibniz and Malebranche (and perhaps Locke), who definitely deduced the falsity of any proposition ascribing causal efficacy to finite existents from the proposition asserting absolute determinism, there was no explicit recognition in the writings of the seventeenth-century philosophers of the incompatibility of the two propositions. When they denied the existence of causal efficacy, they usually did so without explicitly recognizing that it was their assertion of determinism that made causal efficacy inadmissible.

PRELIMINARY DEFINITIONS

But the proposition "finite existents are free" implies that finite existents are causally efficacious, as we shall see; and the proposition "finite existents are free" did have religious sanction. The philosophic opposition between freedom and determinism mirrored the opposition between the concept of God's omnipotence and omniscience and man's moral responsibility. One could not safely deny either of these two last "truths." Hence attempts were made to save an emasculated concept of freedom by pruning away all notions of efficacy or power to act, and leaving only passive acceptance of God's goodness.

The failure to comprehend the relations of determinism and causal efficacy was of serious consequence to the determination of the relation between freedom and causal efficacy. It was supposed that the assertion of freedom implied the denial of causal efficacy. It is in this sense that Spinoza[1] and others argue against freedom. But if we examine the systematic conclusions of the philosophers of the seventeenth century, we discover that those who deny freedom also deny causal efficacy. And we may discover that in each case these propositions must be denied because complete determinism has been asserted.

The conclusions reached above depend, of course, on certain meanings of the terms employed, and do not follow if any other meanings are employed. In order to fix the relations of truth and falsity, we must define the terms, and in this task there is no escaping the charge of arbitrary definition if anyone desires to make it. Definitions can only have pragmatic sanction; and this pragmatic sanction cannot be demanded until

[1] B. Spinoza, *Ethics*, I, App., 39.

the conclusion of this investigation is reached. In the meantime we cannot proceed without fixed meanings for our central concepts, and such fixed meanings are not to be found in any philosophic text that I know of. Therefore we may proceed to define the terms we are to employ.

It is possible to define our concepts in terms of one another. In that case we could definitely establish the relations of the truth values of the propositions, but there would remain a justifiable suspicion that we were engaging in mere word play. On the other hand, unless the concepts are defined in terms of one another, it is difficult to see in what sense the relations of the truth values can be fixed. The way out of this difficulty seems to lie in defining one of these concepts ostensively, and the others in terms of it. In this manner we shall establish the significance of the propositions as descriptive of matter of fact, and also we shall have fixed the relation of the truth values. An example will illustrate this procedure and why it is necessary for our purposes. We may decide that being a snark implies being a rhomboid, and being a rhomboid implies being a boojum. In terms of this decision, we may state the relations of the truth values of propositions employing these concepts. Thus "if x is a snark, x is a boojum," etc. But unless there were such things as snarks, rhomboids, and boojums, the whole affair would have interest only as an exercise in symbols. On the other hand, we may begin by defining a snark ostensively (if there are snarks) by pointing out what sorts of existing things we are to call snarks. Then, if we establish the same relation as before between snark, rhomboid, and boojum, various statements about existing things are possible, which statements will have fixed formal relations, i.e. the truth or falsity of one will imply the truth or falsity of another.

Which concept, of the three we are to consider, is to be defined ostensively is again an arbitrary matter. We might choose any one of the three and fix the meaning of the other two in terms of it. However, a certain convenience of expression is to be gained if we select causation. In what sense this is so will appear below.

An event A causes event B, when B results partly from some activity or influence originating in A. I say partly, because there may be other events causally related to B and because there may originate in B some activity not traceable to any prior causes. This is, in effect, the seventeenth-century definition of causation. According to Gibson, "When closely examined, moreover, the ideas of both causality and power are found to involve the idea of active efficiency. For Locke, as for Descartes, the innermost significance of causality is that of the active initiation of change."[1] Leibniz also gives a negative endorsement to this definition. His decision that there is no causal relation between monads means that no activity originating in one monad can influence another.[2]

We secure ostensive definition for the concept of causation by pointing to those regions of experience where active efficiency is immediately given. And if we search our experience for direct evidence of causal action, we find it in the relation of the events which

[1] J. Gibson, *Locke's Theory of Knowledge and its Historical Relations*, 106.
[2] G. W. von Leibniz, *The Monadology and Other Philosophical Writings*, 222–3.

constitute our own conscious life. So much is all that is necessary, but in case the observation of such a relation be regarded as insufficient to constitute ostensive definition, it can be pointed out that both Leibniz and Locke regarded it as satisfactory. "We are abundantly furnished with the idea of passive power by almost all sorts of sensible things.... Nor have we of active power (which is the more proper signification of the word 'power'[1]) fewer instances; since, whatever change is observed, the mind must collect a power somewhere to make that change, as well as the possibility of the thing itself to receive it. But yet if we will consider it attentively, bodies, by our senses, do not afford us so clear and distinct an idea of active power, as we have from the reflection on the operations of our minds.... The idea of the beginning of motion we have only from reflection on what passes in ourselves, where we find by experience that, barely by willing it, barely by a thought of the mind, we can move the parts of our bodies which were before at rest. So that it seems to me we have, from the observation of the operation of bodies by our senses, but a very imperfect idea of active power, since they afford us not any idea in themselves of the power to begin any action, either motion or thought."[2] Leibniz, in commenting on the above passage as reproduced by him in his *New Essays*, adds: "I am always agreed with you that the clearest idea of active power comes to us from the mind. It is also only in things which are analogous to the mind, that is to say, in entelechies, for matter properly speaking shows only passive

---

[1] Active power is taken as identical in meaning with causation.
[2] *Essay*, 164–5.

power."[1] With reference to the passage from Locke it should be remembered that "ideas of reflection" are just as primitive as "ideas of sensation," and that Locke listed "power" under simple ideas. By a simple idea Locke meant that which must be ostensively defined, that is to say, defined with reference to immediate experience.

Our assigned definition will be made more definite if we point out here two notions which it excludes. In the first place, as Locke and Leibniz asserted in the above passages (we mention these two specifically, but we might add the names of every other seventeenth-century philosopher), matter cannot be a cause. However clear it seemed that matter was involved in the transference of motion, it was universally recognized that matter could not originate motion. This may be clearly seen in the statement of the first law of motion, which in one form or another was commonly held to be true during this period. Of course, gravity, considered as an innate property of matter, added complications, but these complications can be disregarded for the present. So far as the question here is concerned, if matter is supposed to have an innate power of originating change, then matter may be a cause in accordance with the terms of our definition. But if a particle of matter be considered as unable to initiate change or activity, then matter cannot be a cause.

In the second place, and this exclusion is historically of great importance, there is nothing in our definition which involves a reference to uniformity or *necessary* connection. And this fact, to those who accept Hume's analysis of the causal situation, may lead to the sup-

[1] *New Essays on the Human Understanding*, 177.

position that our definition is too far from the ordinary definition to be of any importance in philosophic analysis. However, we have shown that Locke and Leibniz accepted definitions very much like, if not identical with, the one we have given. Leibniz, far from regarding uniformity as implied in the notion of causality, finds that uniformity definitely excludes causal influence. (An exception must be made here, if it is God's causality that is being considered.) This comment must be accepted as it stands at present. Exactly why it is so will become clear after we have defined determinism. In Locke's discussion of power there is no reference to either uniformity or necessary connection. "It will be observed that, throughout Locke's treatment of the subject, there is no suggestion that the idea of causality essentially involves that of uniformity or necessary connection according to law, which is now (since Hume) often regarded as its primary implication. The term 'law of nature' still retained for him the theological implications to which, indeed, we must ultimately trace the attempt to unite in a single conception the ideas of active efficiency and uniformity of behaviour."[1]

Actually, as we shall see, the concept of active power and the concept of uniformity exclude one another and cannot be combined in one notion without contradiction. Locke is aware of this situation,[2] since he

[1] J. Gibson, *Locke's Theory of Knowledge*, etc., 109.
[2] Cf. *Remarks upon some of Mr. Norris's books, wherein he asserts F. Malebranche's opinion of our seeing all things in God.* "A man cannot move his arm or his tongue; he has no power: only upon occasion the man willing it, God moves it. Then man *wills*, he does something; or else God upon the occasion of something which he himself did before, produced this will and this action in him. This is the hypothesis that clears doubts, and brings us at last to the religion of Hobbes and Spinoza; by resolving all, even the

believes that Malebranche's denial of causal efficacy implies complete uniformity or necessary connection.

What then may we conclude concerning Hume's statement that power and necessity are synonymous?[1] It cannot be said that Hume is merely giving a nominal definition of the terms he wishes to employ. He explicitly states that, in the usage of the philosophers he is criticizing, necessity is taken as synonymous with power. In the face of this assertion we may only conclude that Hume showed an alarming lack of knowledge concerning the writings of seventeenth-century philosophers (including Locke, whom Hume was supposed to have studied carefully) and that he showed too great a dependence upon the literal words of Malebranche.[2] These two contentions (Hume's ignorance of Locke and dependence upon Malebranche) can be briefly illustrated. For example, in commenting upon Locke's chapter on power, Hume declares: "I believe the most general and most popular explication of this matter is to say, that finding from experience that there are several new productions in matter, such as the motions and variations of the body, and concluding that there must somewhere be a power capable of producing them, we arrive at last by this reasoning at the idea of power and efficacy. But to be convinced that this explication is more popular than

thoughts of men, into an irresistible and fatal necessity." Published in *A Collection of Several Pieces of Mr. J. Locke*, 170.

[1] "I begin with observing that the terms of efficacy, agency, power, force, energy, necessity, connection, and productive quality are nearly all synonymous. . . . By this observation we reject at once all the vulgar definitions which philosophers have given of power and efficacy." *Treatise*, sect. 14, 155.

[2] For a full treatment of the relation of Hume to Malebranche, see R. Church, *A Study in the Philosophy of Malebranche*, and J. Laird, *Hume's Philosophy of Human Nature*.

philosophical, we need but reflect on two very obvious principles. First, that reason alone can never give rise to any original idea...."[1] Now Hume in this passage is either deliberately misrepresenting Locke or completely failing to understand him. Locke would agree without question to Hume's conclusion that reason can never give rise to any original idea, but Locke never for a moment held that reason gave rise to the idea of power. Power was a simple idea of reflection. And although Locke does say that the mind "collects an idea of power" in observing the changes in matter, he adds that this observation of the changes in matter or the reasoning upon such changes is in no sense the source of the idea of power.

If we examine the writings of seventeenth-century philosophers, we find only one thinker who seemingly identified power and necessity, that is to say, used the terms synonymously as Hume charged. This usage is to be found in the writings of Malebranche, and it is made the grounds of an argument denying power to finite existents. "It is evident that all bodies, great and little, have no force to move themselves; a mountain, a house, a stone, a grain of sand, are alike as to that. We have but two sorts of ideas, viz. of spirits and bodies; and as we ought not to speak what we conceive not, so must we only argue from those two ideas. Since therefore our ideas of bodies convinces us that they cannot move themselves, we must conclude that they are moved by spirits. But considering our idea of finite spirits, we see no *necessary connection* betwixt their will and the motion of any body what-

[1] *Treatise*, 150. Hume in a note directs the reader's attention to Locke's chapter on power.

soever; on the contrary, we perceive that there is not nor can be any. Whence we must infer, if we will follow light and reason, that as no body can move itself, so no created spirit can be the true and principal cause of its motion."[1] Malebranche appears not to have shown what he set out to show. He wishes to point out that no finite existent can be a cause since no finite existent has any power or efficacy. He shows that this is the case for bodies, but instead of asking whether spirits have the *power* to move themselves or other things (which obviously they do have),[2] he asks whether we can find any *necessary connection* between any act of will and the movement of a body. We may reply that obviously we cannot, but that this failure to find necessary connection is irrelevant to the argument. The introduction of the notion of necessary connection vitiates the whole argument. The search is supposedly for that which has the power to move bodies, and not for that which is connected necessarily with the motion of bodies. Further, just as we know that no body[3] can move itself, the concept of the soul or spirit involves the power of self-movement (and this in Malebranche's own philosophy up to this point). Malebranche argues here that there is no necessary connection between the will and the movement of a body. But this says nothing about the power of the will to move the body. If he genuinely wishes to deny power, he must prove that it is contradictory or impossible in any case for the movement of the body to be caused by an act of the will. But he does not

[1] F. Malebranche, *Search After Truth*, 55.
[2] Malebranche himself ascribes power to finite spirits in another connection. Ibid., 3.
[3] This follows from the definition of body accepted by Malebranche.

assert this for the obvious reason that if he did he would be talking nonsense.

It may be said at this point that Malebranche had the right, if he wished to exert it, of defining terms as he pleased, and that if he chooses to define power in terms of necessary connection, there can be no disagreement. But it must be remembered, if we allow Malebranche his definition, he is saying nothing about power or efficacy as those words are usually understood. Thus when he argues as follows, "But men are so far from being the true causes of the motions produced in their body, that it seems to imply a contradiction that they should be so. For a true cause is that betwixt which and its effect the mind perceives a necessary connection; for so I understand it. But there is none besides the infinitely perfect being, betwixt whose will and the effects the mind can perceive a necessary connection; and therefore none but God is the true cause or has real power of moving bodies,"[1] there really can be no quarrel. Allowing, for the sake of the argument, that the necessary connection between the will of God and the effects is comprehensible, what is finally asserted is that we can have no other idea of necessary connection. But there is, again, nothing in the argument which gives the slightest reason for the conclusion that finite things lack efficacy or power, if we admit that it is conceivable in any particular case that a particular effect does not follow.[2]

Now the fact that Malebranche restricted necessary connection to the relation between the will of God and

---

[1] *Search After Truth*, 56.

[2] Malebranche's position will be treated with more detail in Chapter II, sect. 4.

the effects, makes Hume's confusion between necessary connection and power doubly reprehensible, since Hume is undoubtedly using the term "power" as it is ordinarily used in reference to finite things. And he might read many more books than he had read at the tender age when he wrote his *Treatise* without discovering any first-rank philosopher who supposed that the power of finite existents manifested itself in necessary connections between finite existents. This is not to say that it was not supposed that there was such necessary connection, but no attempt was ever made to account for it in terms of a finite existent's exercise of power.

We may assume at this point that we have given a meaning to the term "cause." But if we wish to fix the meaning of the proposition "A causes B," we must also decide what sorts of entities A and B stand for. That is to say, we have fixed the meaning of a propositional function, and we must determine what values can be substituted for the variable to form a significant proposition. For example, in the expression "x is red," the class of objects or entities which can be substituted for x is limited. If we substitute "wisdom" for x, the proposition is non-significant. Now there is no logical criterion for the significance of propositions (I am excepting here the law of contradiction). When we assert that "wisdom is red" we are not asserting "$p . - p$," a contradiction. In other words, there is no *a priori* rule which can determine the class of entities which can be substituted for the variable.[1]

[1] To accept as a rule the contemporary dictum that the proposition must not violate the rules of logical grammar is to accept nothing at all. For what we wish to know is the "rule of logical grammar" in this particular case. Thus, if we are told that the expression "wisdom is red" violates the rules of logical grammar, we may ask for the rule which limits

In one respect the law of contradiction will help us at this point. We may rule out in advance (*a priori*) all entities defined in terms of a function which contradicts the function for which we desire to find arguments. We know, by definition, that we cannot substitute for x, in the expression "x is red," entities defined as not-coloured. It was on these grounds that we decided that matter as traditionally defined could not be a cause. In terms of our definition, an entity to be a cause must be able to originate activity. Now if it is part of the definition of matter or atoms that they cannot change without external influences, it follows that we cannot substitute the term "matter" in the expression "x causes y" or "x is a cause." However, if atoms are supposed to be endowed with a power of spontaneous action (e.g. the atoms of Lucretius) atoms might be causes in the required sense.

Generally, we may decide that the kinds of entities which may be causes are acts or events. Thus the proposition "A causes B," where A is an act or an event, may be true or false, but it is significant in either case. However, Locke and Leibniz, to whom we have appealed for confirmation of our definition, believed that power or efficacy belonged to substantial beings. The point here is whether or not there are any acts or events which do not implicate agents which act or substances in which the events inhere. Thus Locke would argue that acts involve an agent which acts, and that activity originates in the agent and not in the act; and Leibniz would hold that appetitions are appetitions of a monad, and that it is the monad,

the class of entities which may be substituted for x, in "x is red." If we are told now that the substitution must be such as not to violate the rules of logical grammar, we are really told nothing.

not any particular appetite, which is the cause of another appetite. It may be thought that the difficulty we are here facing is not serious or genuine, that we might readily accept the substitution of "agents" for "acts" and "substances" for "events" without prejudice to the significance of our proposition. But to do so would be to load our proposition with the whole question of substantial identity. Thus someone who objected to substantial identity, no matter what the reason for his objection, might find the proposition "A is a cause," where A is a substance, meaningless. (This point will be more concretely illustrated in our discussion of freedom.)

We cannot consider here the many reasons, philosophic and otherwise, which led Locke or Leibniz to the decision that acts imply agents. What we can consider is whether or not the experiences in terms of which they ostensively defined causation actually involved an experience of substance. The question put in this form makes the answer obvious. Locke may have supposed on other grounds that the experience of power involved a substantial agent, but in terms of the experience itself no substantial agent is given. Leibniz, too, had empirical evidence for the relation of perceptions or appetitions, but such evidence does not involve the working out of an immortal monad. That is to say, even if it is possible to show that Locke meant nothing by substance, and Leibniz meant nothing by his eternal monads, the empirical fact of power or perceptions of appetition would still remain unquestioned. Hence, following a clue from Hume,[1]

---

[1] Hume says that each perception may be regarded as a substance. *Treatise*, 223.

we may say that each individual act or event is substantial, and that the mind or a monad is nothing but a system of such entities. Thus what is meant by the proposition "the mind is the cause, etc.," is not that some transcendent entity is causally related to other things, but that the system of acts which we call mind is causally responsible for another act. In other words, in restricting the class of things which may be causes to such things as are obviously particular existents, we avoid nominalistic arguments to the effect that the will or mind cannot be causes because they are nothing but names for particular volitions or thoughts.[1]

Our task now is to define the concepts of freedom and determinism in terms of the concept of causation. A finite existent is said to be free when some degree of its activity, however small, is underived from any other existent. We say "existent" rather than "finite existent" because we wish to exclude the possibility of the kind of freedom which Leibniz attributed to his monads. The activity of any particular monad was underived so far as any other finite monad was concerned, but the monad could not be considered free in terms of our definition, since the activity of every monad was derived from God, or an infinite being.

It will be seen that this definition of freedom is identical with our definition of causation, except that the latter contains a reference to an effect. Thus when we say that the activity of a finite existent is underived, we are really saying that power or activity originates in this finite existent. Hence the statement "A causes B" implies that A is free. If it is true that "A causes B," it is also true that "A is free." The two propositions,

[1] See below.

however, are not equivalent, since if "A is free" is true it does not follow that "A is the cause of B" is true. For B might result from the activity of finite existents exclusive of A. On the other hand, if we deny the consequent we must deny the antecedent. Thus if "A is free" is false, then "A causes B" is also false.

It should also be noticed, and this is of paramount importance, that the proposition "A causes B" says nothing about whether or not B is free. In our definition of causation we said only that the proposition "A causes B" means that B results *in part* from an activity originating in A. An activity might originate in B not caused by A or anything else. Hence the proposition "B is free" is compatible with the proposition "A causes B."

What was said above concerning the kind of entities that could be causes must be said again with regard to the kind of entities that can be free. During the Middle Ages the question of freedom emerged as a consequence of the controversy over the relative importance of the will and intellect.[1] Hence the question, as it was inherited by the seventeenth century, was not *Are individuals free?* (here *individual* is used in the sense of a particular existent) but *Is the will free?* This was unfortunate, because it imported into the problem a great deal of dubious psychology, and questions as to freedom usually resolved themselves into questions as to the nature of the will and its relations to ideas supplied by the intellect.[2] Locke attributed most of the confusion on the question of freedom to this improper question. "*Liberty belongs not*

[1] W. Windelband, *A History of Philosophy*, 328.
[2] Cf. the Leibniz-Clarke correspondence.

to the will. If this be so (as I imagine it is), I leave it to be considered, whether it may not help to put an end to that long-agitated, and I think unreasonable, because unintelligible question, viz. Whether man's will be free or no? For, if I mistake not, it follows from what I have said that the question itself is altogether improper; and it is as insignificant to ask whether man's will be free as to ask whether his sleep be swift, or his virtue square: liberty being as little applicable to the will as swiftness of motion is to sleep, or squareness to virtue . . . and when anyone well considers it, I think he will as plainly perceive that liberty which is but a *power*, belongs only to agents, and cannot be an attribute or modification of the will, which is also but a power."[1]

This question, *Is the will free?* seemed to imply that a decision as to the nature of the will carried with it an answer to the question of freedom. Locke, as we have seen, tried to separate the question,[2] but others who did not so separate them made an attack on the concept of the will the basis for an attack on freedom. The demonstration that "will" is just a name for particular volitions forms an important part of Spinoza's argument for determinism. It is used in the *Ethics*,[3]

[1] *Essay*, 169. I have indicated previously my disagreement with Locke on the question of the nature of agents. Any event or act can be regarded as an agent, and any event or act can have *power* in the sense required for freedom.

[2] "*Power belongs to agents*. It is plain then that the will is nothing but one power or ability, and freedom another power or ability: so that to ask whether the will has freedom is to ask whether one power has another power. . . . For who is it that sees not that powers belong only to agents . . ." It may be seen from this passage that the question of the relations of an agent to a will is distinct from the question of the freedom of agents. Ibid., 169–70.

[3] *Ethics*, Book II, Prop. 49, corr.

and more specifically in a letter to Oldenburg.[1] "Therefore, taking little notice of the other reasons which are of no moment, I will show that this reason (that the will is the cause of error) is false, a fact which they, too, would easily have seen if they had only paid attention to this, namely, that will differs from this or that volition in the same way as whiteness differs from this or that white thing, or humanity differs from man; so that it is just as impossible to conceive that the will is the cause of this or that volition as that humanity is the cause of Peter and Paul. Since, therefore, will is nothing but a thing of reason and cannot be said to be in any way the cause of this or that volition, and particular volitions since they need a cause in order to exist, cannot be said to be free, but are necessarily what they are determined to be by their causes, and lastly, since, according to Descartes, these errors are particular volitions, it necessarily follows that errors, that is, particular volitions, are not free but are determined by external causes, and in no way by the will."[2]

Here the denial of freedom follows directly from the proof that there is no such thing as the will. It is true that in Descartes' description of the cause of error he used the phrase "freedom of the will." But Descartes was a good deal of a medievalist, and freedom to him meant determination by the will. However, what he intended to convey was only that the power of judging was underived, and he might have said that we err because particular volitions are free. Had he done so, Spinoza's nominalistic argument

[1] Here is the concrete illustration promised above. Cf. page 28.
[2] B. Spinoza, *Correspondence*, edited by A. Wolf, 77-8.

would have left his position untouched. (Spinoza elsewhere attacked the notion that individual volitions are free, but what he has to say in the above passage would be irrelevant in such an attack.) Whatever else they may be, volitions are acts or events, and thus the proposition "A is free," where A is a particular volition, is significant.

If we regard any proposition which asserts freedom as q, then the assertion of determinism is the assertion of not-q. Thus the proposition "A is determined" means that it is false that "A is free." If we substitute the active form of the verb, the proposition "A determines B" means that B is not free. So far as this definition goes, no meaning is given to the expression "A determines . . ." other than that the entity determined cannot be free. I shall discuss the significance of "A determines . . ." after I have fixed the relationship of determinism to freedom and causation.

We have said that if "A is free" is true then "A is determined" is false; and since the negation of not-q is q, if "A is determined" is false, then "A is free" is true. It follows further that since "A determines B" is equivalent to "B is determined by A" that if "A determines B" is true, then "B is free" is false. Now since "A causes B" implies "A is free," "A causes B" and "A is determined" cannot both be true. (Keeping the assigned notation q and not-q, and substituting p for "A causes B," we have p implies q implies not both p and not-q.) If "A is determined" is false it does not follow that "A causes B" is true, since "A causes B" does not follow from "A is free." If "A is determined" is true, then "A causes B" must be false; and if "A causes B" is true, then "A is determined" is false.

PRELIMINARY DEFINITIONS

And, finally, if "A determines B" is true, "B is free" is false; but if "A causes B" is true, then "B is free" *may* be true also. As we shall see, this last implication is of great importance. For example, in the passage from Spinoza quoted above, there is the statement "and particular volitions since they need a cause in order to exist, cannot be said to be free." In terms of the meaning we have given to "cause" this is a *non sequitur*. On the other hand, if Spinoza means here by "cause" what we mean by "determines," then he is saying merely that since particular volitions are not free, they are not free. It will be said, of course, that Spinoza means by "determines" not only the negation of freedom as we have defined it, but the inconceivability of any particular volition not following from its cause. In other words, it will be said that Spinoza is here affirming the existence of necessary connection.

The proposition "A determines B" not only means that B is not free, but also that A and B are necessarily connected in the sense that, given A, it is inconceivable that B shall not follow. The notion of necessary connection enters into the concept of determinism when the latter is generalized. Thus, if no entity is free, then every entity is determined. But if every entity is determined, then no entity can be a cause; and the proposition "A determines B" cannot express a causal activity on the part of A. In the universal denial of freedom, determinism is left without the possibility of accounting for causal connections. In order to give significance to the causal relation, determinism must add a reference to a free existent capable of causal action; and this free existent for most of the seventeenth-century philosophers is God. If no entity can be the cause of anything, then God must be the cause of everything. Now since God is the cause of everything, it is inconceivable that anything can be other than it is or fail to follow from His activity in just the manner that it does follow. If God is the sole cause, there can be no other causes, and everything must be completely determined; but if God is the sole cause, everything must follow necessarily from His activity. It is important to notice that in itself the denial of freedom does not involve necessary connection; but the assertion of necessary connection (consequent on the sole causality of God) does involve a denial of freedom. There might be a deterministic world in which there was no causal action, and in which there were no necessary connections· but in such a world nothing could occur, since there would be no source of action. Thus, in a deterministic world, in order to secure a ground for dynamic relationships, it is necessary to appeal to God's causality as the source of all activity. But God's activity involves necessity; hence a deterministic world in which anything occurred would be a world in which connections were necessary.

The addition of the concept of necessary connection to the concept of determinism does not upset the relations we have exhibited above. Rather it is only the fact that a determined entity is neither free nor a cause that makes possible the addition of necessary connection to the concept of determinism. As we shall see, it is impossible to assert that necessary connection holds between free existents (below, Chapter III, page 118 f.) Henceforth, then, I shall regard the proposition "A determines B" as asserting, not only that B is not free, but that A and B are necessarily connected. Conversely, I shall regard the proposition "A is not-free" as implying that A is involved in a system of necessary connections.[1]

Whether any denial of freedom which implies the assertion of necessary connection can be made comprehensible is of course questionable. I shall try to show conclusively that, lacking an appeal to God, such a denial cannot be made comprehensible. However, if once we grant the existence of a God defined in terms of omniscience, omnipotence, etc., necessary connection not only becomes comprehensible, but propositions asserting it must be regarded as true. And no propositions bearing upon the relation of finite existents advanced by the philosophers of the seventeenth century can be understood if it is divorced from the proposition universally accepted, namely, God (defined as omnipotent and omniscient) exists.

In the chapters that follow we shall be concerned to establish the truth or falsity, not of particular propositions which hold that "A or B or C is determined," but of the proposition which asserts complete or universal determinism. Now it may be said that in ostensively defining causation I designated at least one

[1] The paradoxes which arise from the assertion of complete determinism or necessary connection will be exhibited in detail in the chapters which follow. It is sufficient here to indicate their nature. If all entities are determined, then no entities are free; if no entities are free, then none can be causes. What then can be said concerning the manner in which God's activity is transmitted throughout the world? Ultimately, all relations must have their ground in God's activity. Thus when we assert that "A determines B" what is really meant is that God, acting through A, causes B. In this conclusion we have the source of the "pre-established harmony" and the doctrine of occasional causes.

case where the proposition "A causes B" is true. But if in even one case the proposition "A causes B" is true, then the proposition "All things are determined" must be false. It would appear, then, that we have prejudiced our investigation from the start. We intend to determine the truth or falsity of a proposition which must at the outset be considered false if what has been said so far is accepted. However, those who assert determinism are not so easily routed. They may have many reasons for believing in the truth of the proposition "All things are determined," and, confronted with the experience which ostensively defines causation, they may always hold that the experience is illusory. In other words, they may argue that "cause" can be ostensively defined and that we may know what we mean by the proposition "A causes B"; but they may add that, for other weighty reasons, the experience of causation is illusory and that in every case the proposition "A causes B" is false. This is in effect the procedure of determinists like Spinoza[1] and Hume.[2] Both find that immediate experience attests to the truth of freedom and hence to the falsity of determinism, but both argue that this immediate experience is not trustworthy. Descartes also faces the difficulty of reconciling the experience of freedom with the truth of determinism, but his conclusion differs from that of Spinoza or Hume. Descartes believes that the experience of freedom is indubitable: *"That the freedom of the will is self-evident. Finally, it is so evident that we are possessed of a free will that can give or withhold its assent, that this may be counted as one of the first and most ordinary notions that are found*

---

[1] *Ethics*, I, App. 39. [2] *Treatise*, II, 121.

innately in us."[1] But, on the other hand, he holds: *"That we likewise know certainly that everything is pre-ordained by God.* But because that which we have already learned about God proves to us that His power is so immense that it would be a crime for us to think ourselves ever capable of doing anything which He had not already ordained, we should soon be involved in great difficulties if we undertook to make His pre-ordinances harmonize with the freedom of our will and if we tried to comprehend them both at the same time."[2]

Here we have contradictory assertions, and Descartes is quite right in saying that we shall get into difficulties if we try to hold both at the same time. But he does not wish to give up either, and the next principle suggests what Descartes thinks may be a solution. *"How the freedom of the will may be reconciled with Divine pre-ordination.* Instead of this we shall have no trouble at all if we recollect that our thought is finite, and the omnipotence of God, whereby He has not only known from all eternity that which is or can be, but also willed and pre-ordained it, is infinite. In this way we may have intelligence enough to come clearly and distinctly to know that this power is in God, but not enough to comprehend how He leaves the free action of man indeterminate; and, on the other hand, we are so conscious of the liberty and indifference which exists in us, that there is nothing that we comprehend more clearly and perfectly. For it would be absurd to doubt that which we inwardly experience and perceive as existing within ourselves, just because we do not comprehend a matter which

[1] R. Descartes, *Works*, I, *Principles*, Pt. I, princ. 39, 234–5.
[2] Ibid., princ. 40, 235.

from its nature we know to be incomprehensible."[1] That is, we know from the nature of the propositions that the combined truth of both is incomprehensible; but, since we wish to give up neither, we must lay the difficulty at the door of our human frailty or finite intelligence. This is no solution, but what else may Descartes offer? He can either deny that he experiences what he does experience or quarrel with the Church; and Descartes was too honest to do the former and too clever to do the latter. If the opposition between freedom and determinism had remained an opposition between something experienced and theological authority its significance might be minimized. But it was translated into an opposition (as we shall see) between the experience of contingency and the demands of deductive science.

There is one last point which must be made before this chapter is concluded. I have said that my definitions are arbitrary, and yet I have been concerned to point out the agreement of my assigned meanings with traditional meanings in an effort to show that the meanings I have assigned were current in the seventeenth century. However, I have conceded that my definitions are arbitrary in order to avoid criticism such as the following: Someone will point out that on page "so-and-so" Locke states that *matter is the cause* of our sensations. Although I think it can be shown that Locke did not mean essentially what he appears to say here, and that he really held the relationship between matter and sensation to be incomprehensible, in stating that our definition is arbitrary I avoid such side excursions. I should say merely that Locke in this passage is not using "cause" as I have defined it.

[1] R. Descartes, *Works*, I, *Principles*, Pt. I, princ. 41, 236.

CHAPTER II

THE ARGUMENTS FOR DETERMINISM IN SEVENTEENTH-CENTURY PHILOSOPHY

IT is sometimes the case that a conclusion, accepted because certain premises upon which it is seen to rest are accepted, attains through the influence of custom and habit a degree of plausibility in its own right. That is, we may believe that A is true because we know that B and C are true. At a later date we may cease to believe B or C, or, what is more likely, forget that we ever believed them. Nevertheless, we may still continue to believe that A is true. This tendency to retain a conclusion after the arguments upon which it rests have been given up is a common and, many believe, a pernicious phenomenon. For example, the existence of frontiers may be advanced as the reason why unrestricted individual economic activity is desirable. And even when there are no more frontiers people may continue to believe that such activity is desirable, which, of course, it may be, and that independently of any justification in terms of the existence of frontiers. But if the existence of frontiers is the only reason why one should believe that certain kinds of behaviour are desirable, then the absence of frontiers leaves us without any reason for the belief. However, when the premises upon which any conclusion depends have been discarded or are no longer believed, the desire to retain the conclusion can lead to a search for other premises. Although psychologically we can condemn such a procedure as rationalization, logically the new argument may be every bit as satisfactory as the old. These considerations make it possible to limit definitely the scope of this chapter. I shall not be concerned with the question of the truth or falsity of the conclusions; nor with what arguments in general might be advanced to support them; nor with the validity of specific arguments. My only object is to discover the arguments which actually led certain thinkers to certain conclusions. But here another qualification must be inserted. I am well aware of the fact that all sorts of psychological and sociological factors may be advanced as the reason for certain beliefs or conclusions, and that explicit reasons may not be the psychological and sociological causes which led any particular individual to conclusions explicitly asserted. Thus it may be that Descartes was led to the conclusion that God is the efficient cause of everything that happens[1] because he feared a possible repetition of the indignity which Galileo had endured. It may be that Leibniz's doctrine of the "pre-established harmony" arose from his desire to conciliate Protestantism and Catholicism. But it should be obvious that one can only speculate upon such reasons or hidden premises, and that investigation must confine itself to the explicit statement of premises.

The issue here will be completely clarified if a distinction is made between logical and psychological reasons. We have a logical reason to believe A, when the truth of A follows necessarily from the truth of B, and B is believed. It should be noticed that I have excluded from the class of logical reasons all cases in which the truth of B makes it only probable that A is true. This exclusion implies no decision as to the

[1] R. Descartes, *Works*, I, *Principles*, Pt. I, princ. 28.

nature of probability judgments, but only that I shall not consider them. A psychological reason for believing something can be defined as any reason unrelated to the question of truth or falsity.[1]

More concretely, my purpose in this chapter is to illustrate the fact that when certain seventeenth-century philosophers asserted the truth of determinism and the falsity of freedom, these assertions followed as conclusions from premises asserting the existence of God and describing His relation to the world. I say "certain philosophers" when I might have said "the important philosophers." But such a judgment, although it may have the full weight of accepted critical opinion as a support, is really unnecessary. I propose to consider the argument for determinism as it appears in the writings of Hobbes, Descartes, Spinoza, Leibniz, and Malebranche. Now there are undoubtedly important names omitted from this list, but none of those omitted are names of explicit determinists.

Except when necessary for purposes of exposition, I shall reserve all comparison of the arguments as used by each individual until the last section of this chapter. Little actual comparison will be necessary, since the similarity of the arguments will be apparent in the statement of them.

Section I.—THE ARGUMENT FOR DETERMINISM IN DESCARTES

As we have seen (Chapter 1), Descartes believed that a consideration of the nature of God and His relation

---

[1] A psychological "reason" is obviously a causal influence and not a "reason" at all. I omit this distinction from the body of the text because I have not yet shown that there is anything like causal influence.

to the world led necessarily to the assertion of determinism. It is not merely a belief in God that makes a man a determinist; Locke and Newton were undoubtedly more pious than Descartes, yet they cannot be called determinists. Only when the proposition that God is omniscient and omnipotent becomes a basic tenet of a philosophic system is it implied that determinism is asserted in such a system.

Descartes' discussion of the relation of God to the world can be divided into two parts: first, the proof of God's existence based upon a consideration of the nature of finite substance and time; second, the conclusions concerning the connection of entities in the world once God's existence has been demonstrated. Under the first division I shall not consider Descartes' use of the ontological argument, since this argument, although it tells us something of God's nature, namely, that He is infinite and perfect, does not in itself contain a reference to the relation of God to the world. This last is the province of the causal argument.[1]

In his version of the causal argument Descartes does not depend upon the usual difficulty of an infinite regress: "Firstly, then, I have not drawn my arguments from observing an order or succession of efficient causes in the realm of sensible things. . . ."[2] Instead he depends on the independence of successive moments of time. This independence requires, he

---

[1] I call the argument drawn from the nature of finite substance and time the causal argument. I shall not consider the argument for God's existence based upon the assertion that "there must be as much reality in the effect as the cause." Whatever the decision concerning the validity of this argument or "proof," the conclusions reached in this section will not be affected.

[2] *Works*, II, 12.

believes, a ground of connection in order that any finite substance can endure through successive moments. "For all the course of my life may be divided into an infinite number of parts, none of which is in any way dependent on the other; and thus from the fact that I was in existence a short time ago it does not follow that I must be in existence now, unless some cause, so to speak, produces me anew, that is to say, conserves me. It is as a matter of fact perfectly clear and evident to all those who consider with attention the nature of time that, in order to be conserved in each moment in which it endures, a substance has need of the same power and action as would be necessary to produce and create it anew, supposing it did not yet exist; so that the light of nature shows us clearly that the distinction between creation and conservation is solely a distinction of reason."[1] It seems plain that what Descartes means here by the independence of moments of time is only that from the existence of a substance at any one moment its existence at any subsequent moment does not necessarily follow. (" . . . it does not follow that I *must* be in existence . . .") This point becomes clearer in Descartes' reply to Gassendi. Gassendi had argued that the moments of time are necessarily connected in the sense that any given moment is necessarily followed by another. To this argument Descartes answers: "This can plainly be demonstrated from what I explained about the independence of the parts of time, which you in vain attempt to elude by propounding the necessary character of the connection between parts of time considered in the abstract. Here it is not a question of

[1] *Works*, I, 168.

abstract time, but of the time or duration of something which endures; and you will not deny that the single moments of this time can be separated from their neighbours, i.e. that a thing which endures through individual moments *may* cease to exist...."[1] Here it is apparent that what Descartes means by the independence of the moments of time is that it is conceivable that anything which exists may cease to exist. But Descartes is not content with any possibility of a thing existing or ceasing to exist. He requires some ground for asserting that successive stages of existence are dependent upon one another, that is, that what follows any one moment of existence is necessarily determined. Now Descartes was completely aware that necessary connection between successive moments of time or of existence could only be grounded in God Himself. That is, the only Being who can secure necessary connection between existents is a being capable of creating or annihilating the world, that is to say, God.

In asserting that the distinction between creation and conservation is only a distinction of reason, Descartes is supposed to have laid the foundation of occasionalism. I can find in the above passages no explicit denial of causal efficacy. The conclusion that God determines everything that happens and all connections between happenings does, of course, imply the denial of causal efficacy. But the point is whether or not this denial was implied in Descartes' doctrine of the independence of successive moments of time. I do not think this denial is so implied if, as seems clear, Descartes meant by "independence" only the absence of necessary connection (". . . it does not follow that I

[1] *Works*, II, 219. Italics mine.

must be in existence . . ."). But from this definition of independence it does not follow that it is "perfectly clear and evident to all those who consider with attention the nature of time" that there are *no* relations between successive moments. Causal influence is one relation, at least, which does not imply necessary connection. It is conceivable that I shall die to-morrow, but it is also true that if I live I shall carry with me some of the influence of to-day. If we suppose Descartes really to mean that there is no connection or relation of any kind between my life now and my life two minutes hence, then we suppose Descartes to be meaning nonsense. However, as I have said, the conclusion that all things and all moments are necessarily connected because God is the ground of their connection, does imply a denial of causal efficacy. If what happens is a result of God's activity, it cannot be the result of causal influence or activity on the part of finite things.

This conclusion, that finite activity is incompatible with necessary connection based upon the constant activity of God, brings us to the second part of our discussion of Descartes (see page 42). Descartes, unlike Malebranche, had no intention of denying finite efficacy; he wishes only to establish necessary connection. That he virtually denied it was recognized by the Occasionalists; but it must not be supposed that, for either Descartes or Malebranche, the inconceivability of finite efficacy was a premise or the first step. This point cannot be too strongly emphasized, and the failure to understand it is responsible for a good deal of the muddle which invests the concept of causation. For example, Norman Kemp Smith, in commenting upon the Cartesian source of occasionalism, says: "If finite bodies have so little hold on reality that they require at each moment to be recreated, they cannot be capable of causing changes in one another: not having sufficient reality to persist, they cannot have sufficient force to act...."[1] Now this is not Descartes' explicit position. He repeatedly speaks of the causal activity of particular existents.[2] But the causal activity of finite existents cannot give rise to any necessary connections and, further, is opposed to determinism. Hence Descartes holds that finite entities are recreated from moment to moment, not because it is inconceivable that they may exist from moment to moment, but because their connection from moment to moment cannot be necessary unless God does re-create them. God is required, not because finite entities have not the power to act, but because necessary consequences cannot be supposed to follow from this power alone. To be sure, once we have concluded that God's power and conservation (i.e. re-creation) accounts for all things, we find that we have ruled out finite efficacy, but the denial of finite efficacy is not a premise in Descartes' argument.

The evidence supporting the alternative interpretation, i.e. that Descartes began with a denial of causal efficacy, seems to me limited to the following passage: "The present time has no causal dependence on the

[1] N. K. Smith, *Studies in Cartesian Philosophy*, 73–4.

[2] It is true that for Descartes bodies cannot act, but this inability to act is implied in the definition of body as sheer extension, and does not follow from the inability of bodies to persist. Descartes in his arguments for the necessity of God's continual re-creation does not refer to "bodies" but to the moments of his own life, or quite generally to "things." The indubitability of human freedom implies that some entities indubitably "have sufficient force to act."

time immediately preceding it. Hence in order to secure the continued existence of a thing no less a cause is required than that needed to produce it at first."[1] But here Descartes obviously repeated in an attenuated form the same argument used in his *Meditations* and in his reply to Gassendi. This being so, we may conclude that in this passage he does not mean abstract time,[2] and that by the lack of "causal dependence" he means the lack of "necessary connection." Also, in spite of the attempt at clear axiomatic statement, the phrase "secure the continued existence of a thing" is ambiguous. If what is meant is that the continued existence of a thing shall be necessary or determined, then God is indeed required to secure it. But God is not required to insure the passage of causal efficacy. In his answer to Gassendi, where we may suppose Descartes to have been particularly careful, he does not say that the independence of moments of time implies that it is impossible for anything to endure through successive moments. He says only that "a thing which endures through individual moments may cease to endure." And if it may cease to endure, then it may also continue to endure. As we have said, God is required only to make whatever happens necessary.

In short, the argument for the existence of God based upon the independence of moments of time says nothing at all about causation. It starts with the recognition of the absence of necessary connection and holds that God can be the only ground of necessary connection. That is, A does not determine B, but both A and B

---

[1] R. Descartes, *Works*, II, 56.
[2] He concedes to Gassendi the necessary connection of moments of time considered in the abstract.

are determined by C. However, according to our definition, if C determines A and B, then neither A nor B can be causes. But Descartes did not perceive this implication, or at least did not draw it consistently.

The failure to draw this implication consistently is evident in two aspects of Descartes' writings; first, his attempt to relegate God to the status of a general cause and to regard moving bodies as particular causes: "*That God is the primary cause of motion; and that He always preserves the same quantity of motion in the universe.* After having adverted to the nature of motion it is necessary to consider its cause, and that twofold: firstly, the universal and primary, which is the general cause of all motions in the world; and, secondly, the particular, by which it happens that each of the parts of matter acquires the motion which it had not before. And with respect to the general cause, it seems manifest to me that it is none other than God Himself who, in the beginning, created matter along with motion and rest, and now by His ordinary concourse alone preserves in the whole the same amount of motion and rest that He placed in it."[1] However, this passage, in effect, reduces particular causes to occasional causes on the ground that God only can insure the constancy of motion in the universe. The reason why a particular motion B follows a particular motion A does not lie in A but in God. Otherwise it is conceivable that the movement of B shall not follow from A and that the amount of motion in the universe varies. Hence, as Descartes' successors perceived, particular motions must be reduced to the status of occasional causes, that is to say, ultimately there are no particular causes.

[1] R. Descartes, *Works*, I, *Principles*, Pt. 3, princ. 36.

The second inconsistency is more serious. Descartes, as we all know, regarded minds as free and as particular causes while recognizing the supposed truth of the contradictory assertion, namely, that all things are determined (preordained) by God. His advice (see Chapter I, page 37) to hold both beliefs without trying to understand their relations cannot be taken when the relation of the mind to the body is considered. It is all very well to believe in a deterministic physics and at the same time hold that the mind is free, but when we leave physics for physiology we must make some statement as to the relation of minds to the movement of bodies. Descartes' attempt to admit a relation and at the same time to hold fast to determinism is well known, and was shown to be a quibble by Leibniz. Descartes supposed that the mind could not change the quantity of motion but that it could change the direction of motion. But, as Leibniz argued, the laws of physics hold that the direction of motion is determined.[1] Therefore, if it is supposed that minds can change the direction of motion, it is supposed that minds can interfere with physical laws. Descartes, in this position, must say either that minds as free agents break down the deterministic scheme which God has established in the sphere of bodies, or he must hold that the deterministic scheme includes minds. He wished to say neither, so he took refuge in the traditional appeal to the finite nature of our understanding.

[1] G. W. Leibniz, *The Monadology and Other Philosophical Writings*, tr. by Robert Latta, 327–8, and note 30, 328.

Section 2.—THE ARGUMENT FOR DETERMINISM IN HOBBES

In examining Hobbes' doctrine of determinism it is not necessary to collect references from different works. In his controversy with Dr. Bramhall, Bishop of Derry, a clear and completely worked-out doctrine is presented. It is fortunate also that the Bishop of Derry was acute enough to perceive and press the real question at issue. As a result, non-essentials and vituperations are gradually eliminated and we are left with a straightforward statement of opposing positions. I shall not be concerned with the arguments of the Bishop of Derry in themselves, but only as they aid in understanding the position of Hobbes.[1]

A clear statement of the issue is given at the outset of the controversy. "The question in general is stated by the Bishop himself . . . Whether all events, natural, civil, moral, be predetermined extrinsically and inevitably . . . I agree with him in the state of the question."[2] But, in the first exchange of opinions, Dr. Bramhall holds that Hobbes confuses extrinsic necessitation with hypothetical necessitation. Dr. Bramhall argues that the will is free or that men are free because any particular act of will or determination of the mind is not antecedently necessary or *extrinsically* determined. Hobbes, Dr. Bramhall charges, desires to show that the will or the mind is extrinsically determined but that Hobbes' arguments assert only an hypothetical necessity. "But T. H. may say that our

[1] The references are all from Hobbes' *Works*, v, "The Questions Concerning Liberty, Necessity, and Chance, clearly stated and debated between Dr. Bramhall, Bishop of Derry, and Thomas Hobbes of Malmesbury."
[2] Op. cit., 2.

several and respective deliberations and affections are in part the cause of our contrary resolutions, and do concur with the outward causes to make up one total and adequate cause to the necessary production of the effect. If it be so, he hath spun a fair thread, to make all this stir for such a necessity as no man ever denied or doubted of. When all the causes have actually determined themselves, then the effect is in being; for though there be a priority in nature between the cause and the effect, yet they are together in time. And the old rule is, 'Whatsoever is, when it is, is necessarily so as it is.' This is no absolute necessity but only upon supposition, that a man hath determined his own liberty. When we question whether all occurrences be necessary, we do not question whether they be necessary when they are, nor whether they be necessary *in sensu composito*, after we have resolved and finally determined what to do; but whether they were necessary before they were determined by ourselves, by or in the precedent causes before ourselves, or in the exterior causes without ourselves."[1] In other words, Dr. Bramhall recognizes that if we mean by the total or complete cause the cause together with the effect, it is obvious (and indisputable) that, given the cause, the effect is also necessarily given.

Much later in the argument the Bishop of Derry brings a similar charge, and I shall point out lower down the type of proof used by Hobbes which is responsible for it. But whatever arguments Hobbes used in order to establish the truth of determinism or necessity, it is certain that he thought he was saying much more than the Bishop of Derry thought he said.

[1] Op. cit., 31–2.

For his answer to the Bishop on this point leaves no room for any doubt as to the kind of necessity Hobbes wished to assert. "This and that which followeth, is talking to himself at random, till he come to allege that which he calleth an old rule, which is this: 'Whatever is, when it is, etc. . . .' If the bishop think that I hold no other necessity than that which is expressed in that old foolish rule, he neither understandeth me, nor what the word necessary signifieth. Necessary is that which is impossible to be otherwise, or that which cannot possibly otherwise come to pass. Therefore necessary, possible, and impossible have no signification in reference to time past or time present, but only to time to come. His necessary and his *in sensu composito* signify nothing; my necessary is a necessary from all eternity. . . ."[1] And further: "The Bishop might easily have seen that the necessity I hold is the same necessity that he denies; namely, a necessity of things future, that is, an antecedent necessity derived from the very beginning of time. . . . I know as well as he that the cause when it is adequate as he call it or entire, as I call it, is together in time with the effect. But for all that, the necessity may be and is before the effect, as much as any necessity can be."[2]

Once it is understood what Hobbes means by necessity, his manner of demonstrating that all things are determined or necessary presents little difficulty. Whereas, in considering Descartes, I found it necessary to interpret various passages in order to exhibit the nature of the demonstration, Hobbes' position is so apparent that I need only repeat his own words. He was so much the rationalist and so firm in his con-

[1] Op. cit., 35. [2] Op. cit., 48.

viction of the truth of the doctrines he asserted that he stated his conclusions syllogistically and sometimes added the flourish of the "Q.E.D."

All things are necessary because, and only because, there exists a God with the attribute of prescience or foreknowledge. "... from another of God's attributes, which is His foreknowledge, I shall evidently derive that all action whatsoever, whether they proceed from the will or from fortune, were necessary from eternity. For whatsoever God foreknoweth shall come to pass, cannot but come to pass, that is, it is impossible it should not come to pass or otherwise come to pass than it was foreknown. But whatever was impossible should be otherwise, was necessary; for the definition of necessary is, that which cannot possibly be otherwise. ... And whereas they that distinguish between God's prescience and His decree, say the foreknowledge maketh not the necessity without the decree, it is little to the purpose. It sufficeth me, *that whatsoever was foreknown by God, was necessary: but all things were foreknown by God,* and therefore *all things were necessary*. And as for the distinction of foreknowledge from decree in God Almighty, I comprehend it not. They are acts co-eternal, and therefore one."[1]

There is no need to comment upon the main argument of this passage. It states explicitly the thesis I am maintaining (cf. page 41). Nor is it an isolated or exceptional argument with Hobbes. What he says in this place he repeats constantly throughout the entire controversy.[2] The question of the relation of God's

[1] Op. cit., 18-19. Italics mine.
[2] Parallel passages to the above: "On the other side from this position, that a man is free to will, it followeth that the prescience of God is quite taken away. For how can it be known beforehand what man shall have a

foreknowledge to His decrees requires some explanation. Dr. Bramhall would not deny the foreknowledge of God. But he makes a distinction between God's foreknowledge and God's decrees, and holds that things follow of necessity from the latter and not from the former. Hobbes in the above passage refuses to allow the distinction, but in a later passage he himself makes it for an obvious reason. "But that the foreknowledge of God should be a cause of anything cannot truly be said; seeing foreknowledge is knowledge and knowledge dependeth on the existence of things known, and not they on it ..."[1] and further, "that the foreknowledge of God causeth nothing though the will do...."[2] Hobbes is led to make this distinction between God's knowledge and His will (or decree), although it contradicts what he has pre-

will to, if that will of his proceed not from necessary causes, but that he have in his power to will or not to will? So also those things which are called future contingencies, if they come not to pass with certainty, that is to say, from necessary causes can never be foreknown; so that God's foreknowing shall sometimes be of things that shall not come to pass, which is to say, that His foreknowledge is none; which is a great dishonour to the all-knowing power." Op. cit., 17–18. "The like is in the making of a garment; the necessity begins from the first motion towards it which was from eternity, though the tailor and the Bishop are equally insensible to it. If they saw the whole order and conjunction of causes, they would say it were as necessary as anything else can possibly be; and therefore God that sees that order and conjunction, knows it is necessary." Op. cit., 226. "... for God foreknoweth nothing that can possibly not come to pass; but that which cannot possibly not come to pass, cometh to pass of necessity." Op. cit., 212. "To which I could add, if I thought it good logic, the inconvenience of denying necessity; as that it destroys both the decrees and prescience of God almighty. For whatsoever God hath proposed to bring to pass by man as an instrument, or forseeth shall come to pass, a man if he have liberty, such as he (Dr. Bramhall) affirmeth from necessitation, might frustrate and make not to come to pass: and God should either not foreknow it and not decree it, or He should foreknow such things shall be as shall never be, and decree that which shall never come to pass." Op. cit., 428–9.

[1] Op. cit., 105.   [2] Op. cit., 112.

viously said, because he recognizes that an act of knowledge does not create what it knows. Hence the existence of the world is not caused by God's knowledge, but by God's decree or act of creation. And this is the ground upon which Dr. Bramhall makes the distinction. But Hobbes adds a comment, "Knowledge dependeth upon the existence of the thing known," which even Dr. Bramhall would have refused to accept, and one which seems to invalidate his whole argument. If knowledge depends on the existence of the things known, then foreknowledge is by definition impossible. And yet Hobbes rests his whole argument upon the assertion of God's foreknowledge. That the Bishop does not press this point is easily accounted for. He, no more than Hobbes, was prepared to deny the foreknowledge of God. What Hobbes means is that God can foreknow what shall exist only after He has *decreed* what shall exist, and not that God's knowledge must follow the *existence* of things known. If we refuse to accept this interpretation, Hobbes cannot be called a determinist. The point is that if we understand Hobbes to be denying the possibility of foreknowledge, then we must understand him to be denying necessity. Now this is manifestly not what he intended. And his argument from foreknowledge remains unaffected even if we admit a distinction between knowledge and decree. It is only necessary to supply two premises so that the major premise to the syllogism given above —what God foreknows is necessary—can be considered a demonstrated conclusion: What God decreed is necessary; God foreknows whatsoever He decreed; therefore, what God foreknows is necessary.

Since Dr. Bramhall would not and does not refuse

to accept any of the premises of these syllogisms, it seems clear that Hobbes emerges from the controversy triumphant. However, the Bishop does refuse to accept defeat, and ultimately his argument for so refusing is like that of Descartes. We have a clear and distinct idea of our own freedom and also a clear and distinct idea of God's prescience and omnipotence. The difficulty of combining these two ideas is not reason for supposing one of them false. The difficulty signifies merely that our minds are finite. Hobbes feels that it is useless to justify holding contradictory propositions upon the plea that our minds are finite; thus he concludes that everything is necessitated. However, as can be seen from his argument, his conclusion is only effective against someone, like the Bishop of Derry or Descartes, who asserts the fact of divine omnipotence. If, for example, I should assert that I have an immediate intuition of my own freedom, and that I have no intuition of divine omnipotence, then I may refuse to accept the conclusion that everything is determined. Further, Hobbes admits that we can have no knowledge of the way in which God necessitates all things, and that the totality of causes transcends our understanding.[1] Hence his whole argument rests upon a religious dogma.

I have stated above that the argument from the foreknowledge of God is not only an important argument but the only argument used by Hobbes to demonstrate the truth of universal necessity or determinism. However, it is true that Hobbes does present other arguments based upon an analysis of what is meant by a sufficient cause. But, as the Bishop is only

[1] Op. cit., 328 ff.

too eager to point out, in each of these cases Hobbes only succeeds in establishing an hypothetical necessity. And when pressed on this point Hobbes retreats to the safe ground of an appeal to God's foreknowledge. Hobbes holds that if the cause is sufficient[1] it is also necessary; that is, if the sum of conditions is sufficient for the occurrence of an event, then the occurrence of that event is necessary. And he illustrates this contention with an example. "For the seventh point, that all events have a necessary cause, it is there proved in that they have sufficient causes. Further, let us in this place also suppose any event never so casual, as for example, the throwing ambs-ace upon a pair of dice; and see if it must not have been necessary before it was thrown. For, seeing it was thrown, it had a beginning, and consequently a sufficient cause to produce it; consisting partly in the dice, partly in the outwards and in the inward things, as the posture of the party's hand, the measure of force applied by the caster, the posture of the parts of the table and the like. In sum, there was nothing wanting that was necessarily requisite to the production of that particular cast; and consequently the cast was necessarily thrown."[2] To this proof we may answer that if the particular cast was part of the sum of the things wanting to produce the particular cast, then there is no doubt that, given the sum of causes, the effect is also given. And this is the answer to this argument which Dr. Bramhall gives. ". . . our dispute is about absolute necessity; his proofs extend only to hypothetical necessity. Our

[1] By a sufficient cause is meant a cause sufficient to the production of any effect; or a cause, lacking which, the effect cannot be produced.
[2] Op. cit., 406.

question is, whether the concurrence and determination of the causes were necessary before they did occur, or were determined. He proves that the effect is necessary after the causes have concurred and are determined. The freest actions of God or man are necessary by such a necessity of supposition, and the most contingent events that are, as I have plainly showed, (in) No. III, where his instance of ambs-ace is more fully answered. So his proof looks another way from his proposition. His proposition is 'that the casting of ambs-ace was necessary before it was thrown.' His proof is that it was necessary when it was thrown. Examine all his cause over and over, and they will not afford him one grain of antecedent necessity. . . . Now for the credit of his cause let him but name, I will not say a convincing reason nor so much as a probable reason, but even any pretence of reason, how the caster was necessitated from without himself to apply just so much force, neither more nor less. If he cannot, his cause is desperate, and he may hold his peace for ever."[1]

And indeed, in the face of this penetrating analysis advanced by the Bishop (whose thrusts against Hobbes resemble in intelligence those of a later English Bishop against the materialists), Hobbes' position is indeed desperate. But, as we have said, the final victory goes to Hobbes, since he falls back upon the religious dogma that the Bishop must also accept. Hobbes answers: "Another reason, he saith, why my instances are impertinent is because 'they extend only to an hypothetical necessity,' that is, that the necessity is not in the antecedent cause; and thereupon challengeth me for the credit of my cause to name some reason

[1] Op. cit., 412.

'how the caster was necessitated from without himself to apply just so much force to the cast, and neither more nor less; or what necessity there was why the caster must throw on to that table rather than the other, or that the dice must fall just upon that part of the table, before the cast was thrown.' Here again, from our ignorance of the particular causes that concurring make up the necessity, he inferreth that there was no such necessity at all; which indeed is that which has in all this question deceived him, and all other men that attribute events to fortune. But I suppose he will not deny that event to be necessary where all the causes of the cast and their concurrence, and the cause of that concurrence, are foreknown, and might be told him, though I cannot tell him. Seeing therefore God foreknows them all, the cast was necessary; and that from antecedent cause from eternity; which is no hypothetical necessity."[1] And this last is obviously so; an antecedent necessity from all eternity is more than an hypothetical necessity. But the Bishop's challenge still stands; if a reference to God is excluded, Hobbes admits implicitly (cf. above passage) that he can name no reason or give any evidence that all things are necessitated. The Bishop and "all other men" conclude from their ignorance of necessity that things are not necessitated. And lacking the appeal to religious dogma or conviction Hobbes would be forced to the same conclusion.

Section 3.—THE ARGUMENT FOR DETERMINISM IN SPINOZA

In attempting to trace and piece together the deterministic argument in Spinoza I am aware that I shall

[1] Op. cit., 421-2.

be open to the charge of misinterpretation. As in the preceding sections, I shall be concerned to point out that Spinoza concludes that finite existents are determined because they follow from the nature of God in a fixed and necessary manner. But there is no agreement among critics and scholars as to what Spinoza meant by God, or by the notion that finite existents follow in certain specifiable ways from His nature. Since I cannot hope to settle so large an issue here, I can only make clear my own interpretation of this notion, and also make clear what interpretations I am rejecting. The rejection of alternate interpretations in no sense invalidates or weakens the conclusion which I shall draw. For, as I shall try to show, if we suppose Spinoza to have meant by God either of the interpretations which I reject, then we must also suppose that Spinoza did not deny freedom nor affirm determinism or necessary connection in any significant sense.

The two interpretations which I reject are: (1) the notion that by God or Substance Spinoza meant the totality of existing things; and (2) the notion that by God or Substance Spinoza meant the one reality of which all finite entities are delusive appearances.

(1) If by Substance or God is meant nothing but the totality of existing things, then all the statements in the *Ethics* (or other writings) which profess to assert a causal relation between God and particular things become nonsense; and nonsense of a sort which Spinoza himself found particularly distressing. We have seen (Chapter 1) that in considering Descartes' explanation of error Spinoza held all other reasons could be considered of no moment and that one reason alone was

sufficient to demonstrate the absurdity of Descartes' account. Since, according to Spinoza, we mean by the will nothing but a name for particular volitions and by humanity nothing but a name for particular men, it is nonsense to suppose that the will is the cause of particular volitions or that humanity is the cause of particular men. But it follows further, on the same grounds, that Substance or God, being but a name for particular things, cannot be the cause of particular things. Yet Spinoza continually refers to God as the *Cause* of things. Can we suppose that Spinoza committed the error or talked the sort of nonsense which he had particularly pointed out in the writings of another philosopher?

It is impossible, of course, to calculate the percentage of propositions, proofs, and scholia which become nonsense of the sort which Spinoza himself would have undoubtedly recognized if God or Substance is supposed to be only a name for the totality of existing things. Ultimately, for Spinoza, God is the sole real cause; hence if God is but a name the causal relation becomes meaningless. Those who would refuse to accept this conclusion and would assert that Spinoza does supply a ground of connection between finite things independently of any reference to God might offer as evidence: "An individual thing, or a thing which is finite and which has a determinate existence, cannot exist nor be determined to action unless it be determined to existence and action by another cause which is also finite and has a determinate existence; and again, this cause cannot exist nor be determined to action unless by another cause which is also finite and determined to existence and action, and so on *ad infinitum.*"[1] Is Spinoza here asserting a natural order of particular things without grounding that order causally in the nature of God? A consideration of the proof of this proposition will convince us that this is not the case. The demonstration that there is such a determinate series rests upon the statement that "Whatever is determined to existence and action is thus determined by God."[2] It is clear that Spinoza's purpose in this proposition is not to establish the existence of a series of finite existents with causal connections not dependent upon God. What he intended to establish was the distinction between a series of finite existents and the infinite attributes, though both the series of finite existents and the infinite attributes are "produced" by God.[3] Spinoza uses the phrase "follow from" with reference to both the series of finite things and the infinite attributes. But there is a distinction which is made more clear in the scholium of the following proposition, namely, what we are to understand by *"natura naturans"* and *"natura naturata."* "For by *natura naturans* we are to understand that which is in itself and is conceived through itself, or those attributes of substance which express eternal and infinite essence, that is to say, God, in so far as He is considered as a free cause. But by *natura naturata* I understand everything which follows from the necessity of God's nature, or of any one of God's attributes."[4] Thus the series of determinate existents constitutes *"natura naturata."* But *"natura naturata"* is meaningless in divorce from God. Nor can it be supposed that

---
[1] *Ethics,* I, prop. 28.
[2] Ibid., Opening sentence, Demonst. prop. 28.
[3] Ibid., I, Scholium, prop. 28.
[4] Ibid., I, Scholium, prop. 29.

God is the "remote cause" of the series, so that once the series is originated only a reference to a finite thing is necessary to explain the determination of another finite thing. Spinoza explicitly rejects this interpretation of the proposition: "It follows, secondly, that God cannot be properly called the remote cause of individual things, unless for the sake of distinguishing them from the things which He has immediately produced, or rather which follow from His absolute nature (that is, for the sake of distinguishing *natura naturans* from *natura naturata*). For by a remote cause we understand something which is in no way joined to its effect. But all things which are, are in God, and so depend upon Him that without Him they can neither be nor be conceived."[1] Hence, regardless of what term in the series we designate, its existence and action cannot be conceived to depend solely upon the preceding term, but it must also be conceived to be grounded in God. And if we eliminate any reference to God, we eliminate likewise any proof that any finite existent determines any other finite existent.[2]

(2) The second rejected interpretation requires only brief treatment. Determinism, freedom, and causation are relational concepts. That is, the existence of more

[1] *Ethics*, I, Scholium, prop. 28.

[2] In the corollary to prop. 24 Spinoza states this conclusion in a manner reminiscent of Descartes: "Hence it follows that God is not only the cause of the commencement of the existence of things, but also of their continuance in existence." Since I am not aware of any other proposition or statement in Spinoza's writings which can be made the basis for the supposition that the causal relations between finite existents can be understood independently of any reference to God, I propose to consider the assertion made above as substantiated. If God or Substance be considered nothing but a name for the totality of existing things, Spinoza's discussion of the causal relation becomes essentially meaningless.

than one entity is a pre-requisite of their having any significance. Of course, if there existed only one entity, such an entity would be free. But in saying this we would be saying nothing, because no meaning could be given to the proposition which asserted that such an entity was not free. However, in dealing with determinism and causation, we are manifestly dealing with relations. Now, on the interpretation we are considering, ultimately (or "in the end") there is only one real entity, and hence ultimately there are no relations. It follows that on this view determinism and causation are both meaningless.

The distinction between levels or between appearance and reality (*natura naturata* and *natura naturans*) will not help us at this point. It cannot be said that causation and determinism have only meaning on the level of appearance and that when we come to speak of God they have no meaning. For we cannot talk of causation and determinism in the first place without a reference to God. It may be true that at one level we have God and no causation or determinism. But it is not true that at the other level we have causation and determinism without any reference to God. The point is that in discussing what Spinoza says about determinism and causation we are not concerned with sheer appearance, but with the relation of finite existents (they may be called appearances if anyone desires to do so) to an entity distinct from them, namely, God.

The interpretation which I accept has already been indirectly designated. God is considered as a distinct entity related to the world in a certain definite manner. And He has this relation to the world because He is other than the world. This interpretation, of course, runs directly counter to the usual view that Spinoza is a pantheist. But it must not be forgotten that the "usual view" is one advanced by German idealists. Thus Windelband, in discussing the relation of *natura naturans* to *natura naturata*, holds that the relation between them is not that of efficient causation because they are ultimately the same thing. "If in this connection the *natura naturans* is called occasionally[1] also the efficient cause of things, this creative force must not be thought as something distinct from its workings; this cause exists nowhere but in its workings. This is Spinoza's complete and unreserved pantheism."[2] But if the force is not distinct from its workings, then it is identical with its workings, that is, cause and effect are identical. Hence to say that God causes the world is to say that God is identical with the world; and every time Spinoza uses the term cause or determine he must be supposed to mean nothing.

It is only on the interpretation which I have accepted, namely, God as distinct from the world, that it makes sense to consider Spinoza's assertions of determinism or his denial of freedom. And the objections to this interpretation, with the exception of those which rest upon its disagreement with tradition,

---

[1] The injection of this term "occasionally," which operates to cast a slight upon opposing views, should in itself make us suspect Windelband's conclusions. It is true that Spinoza does not often say that *natura naturans* is the cause of *natura naturata*, but the expression that God is the *efficient cause* of all things appears as often if not more often than any other statement I can think of.

[2] W. Windelband, *A History of Philosophy*, 409. My objection to Windelband does not mean that I think there are no statements in the *Ethics* which suggest pantheism. What I cannot accept is the "complete unreserved pantheism."

can only be based upon statements in Spinoza which assert (1) that God is the immanent cause and not the transcendent cause of all things; and (2) that whatever is, is in God. But the proof of the proposition, which states, "God is the immanent, and not the transitive, cause of all things,"[1] follows from Corollary 1, Prop. 16. This corollary asserts: "Hence it follows that God is the efficient cause of all things which can fall under the infinite intellect." The second part of the proof says only that God is not a transitive cause because outside of God nothing can exist. If we dispense with spatial metaphors, this means only that the existence of all things depends upon God. There is nothing in the proposition or the proof which substantiates in any way idealistic pantheism.[2]

There remains one other question of interpretation before we can proceed with a direct presentation of Spinoza's argument. According to the definitions we have accepted, necessity or determinism is opposed to freedom. However, in a letter to Boxel (1674) Spinoza writes: "It seems no less absurd and opposed to reason to suppose that necessary and free are contraries. For no one can deny that God knows Himself and everything else freely, and yet all agree in admitting that God knows Himself necessarily. Thus you seem to make no distinction between coercion or force and necessity. That man desires to live, to love, etc., is

---

[1] *Ethics*, I, prop. 18.

[2] Descartes held that God is the immanent cause of all that happens, and yet cannot be called a pantheist. And Malebranche, who explicitly distinguishes God and the world, holds that the world is in God. In connection with the question of the relation of God to the world see H. A. Wolfson, *The Philosophy of Spinoza*, I, Chapter 9. Wolfson is definitely opposed to pantheistic interpretations of Spinoza.

not a compulsory activity, but it is none the less necessary."[1] There is, of course, a sense in which necessity and freedom are not contraries. Dr. Bramhall pointed out this meaning of necessity and called it an hypothetical or a necessity of supposition. Spinoza might have called it a necessity of definition. Thus God is free because He is not determined by anything outside of Himself; and He knows Himself and other things necessarily because such knowledge is *part of His definition*. Man's desire to live and love may be necessary in the same sense. But it should be noticed that Spinoza does not conclude here that although this type of necessity is different from compulsion that therefore man is free. Because in the case of man we have a necessity defined in terms of external determination. The meaning of freedom and necessity which we have established is also the meaning which Spinoza accepts: "That thing is called free which exists from the necessity of its own nature alone, and is determined to action by itself alone. That thing, on the other hand, is called necessary, or rather compelled, which by another is determined to existence and action in a fixed and prescribed manner."[2]

It matters not for our purposes, however, whether or not the necessity which Spinoza sometimes asserted was only an hypothetical necessity or a necessity of definition. At other times it is unquestionably the case that he spoke of things as necessitated or determined in the sense we have established. In a letter to Schuller, written in the same year as the one quoted above,

---

[1] B. Spinoza, *Correspondence*, translated by A. Wolf, 287.
[2] *Ethics*, I, Def. 7. Our definition takes into consideration differences of degree.

Spinoza holds: "Lastly, I should like your friend who makes these objections to my theory to tell me how he conceives human virtue, which he says arises from the free decision of the mind, together with the pre-ordination of God. For if, with Descartes, he admits that he does not know how to reconcile them, he is endeavouring to hurl against me the weapon by which he has already been pierced."[1] Spinoza recognizes a definite sense of the meanings of freedom and necessity which makes it nonsense to assert the truth of both.

The distinction between the two meanings of necessity and the relation of each to the meaning of freedom can perhaps best be seen from the manner in which Spinoza uses these terms when he is considering the nature of God and how this usage differs when he changes to the consideration of the nature of man. One sort of necessity God and man have in common; that is, certain things follow from God and man by definition of their natures. But besides being necessitated in this sense, God is free, since His activity originates in Himself and not in anything external. On the other hand, man adds to the necessity of definition the character of being completely determined by that which is external.[2]

Propositions about determinism, freedom, or causa-

[1] B. Spinoza, *Correspondence*, 298. Again (ibid., 256–7) in a letter to Ostens (1671) the same argument is used: ". . . what then does he think of his own Descartes, who states that nothing is done by us which has not been pre-ordained by God, or rather that every single moment we are, as it were, created anew by God, and that nevertheless we act with the freedom of the will? This, assuredly, as Descartes himself confesses, no one can understand."

[2] Man, of course, inasmuch as he *is* God is also not necessitated or determined in this second sense, but our premise in this analysis is the supposition of a genuine distinction between God and man. I refer here to idealistic interpretations which identify the "real" part with the whole.

tion are propositions about existing things. *It is nonsense to talk of an essence as being free or determined.* Hence we must distinguish between God as the cause of the essence of things and as the cause of their existence. In a letter to Schuller (1675) Spinoza declares: "In what sense I understand that God is the efficient cause of things, of their essence as well as their existence, I believe I have sufficiently explained in the Ethics, Scholium and Corollary to Prop. xxv, Part 1."[1] This scholium states that God is the cause of things in the same sense as He is the cause of Himself.[2] I find two difficulties presented here: (1) God is the cause of Himself because His essence includes His existence, but the essence of created things does not include existence. Hence God has the role of external cause to created things. (2) There is a plurality of created things, and this fact of plurality involves an external cause. "Hence we must absolutely conclude that all things which are conceived as existing many in number are necessarily produced by external causes and not by the force of their own nature."[3] In the face of these considerations I can only suppose Spinoza to have meant that God is the cause of essence only, in the same sense as He is the cause of Himself. The very wording of the demonstration should make this clear. Spinoza is careful to repeat exactly what has been proved before he writes Q.E.D., and in this case the

---

[1] B. Spinoza, *Correspondence*, 308.

[2] "This proposition (prop. 25) more clearly follows from prop. 16. For from this proposition it follows that from the existence of the divine nature, both the essence of things and their existence must necessarily be concluded, or, in a word, in the same sense in which God is said to be the cause of Himself, He must be called the cause of all things." Scholium, prop. 25.

[3] B. Spinoza, *Correspondence*, 219. From "Letter to Hudde," 1666.

last statement before the Q.E.D. is, "Therefore God is the cause of the essence of things." And He is the cause of the essence of things in the same sense as He is the cause of Himself, because the essence of things are nothing but the attributes of God, and the attributes of God are included in His definition.

If, then, God is not the cause of the *existence* of things in the same sense as He is the cause of Himself, in what sense is He their cause? This question Spinoza, with Hobbes and Descartes, must leave unanswered. God's relation to the world of existing things remains an ultimate mystery.[1] Why, then, it may be asked, is it necessary to say anything about God's causality? To this question there is an answer. Without a reference to God it is impossible to assert that particular things are determined or necessarily connected. Spinoza establishes the truth of determinism or necessary connection in the series of propositions 24 to 29. Proposition 24 with the corollary denies that the necessary existence of anything is conceivable without a reference to God. "Hence it follows that God is not only the cause of the commencement of the existence of things, but also of their continuance in existence. . . . For if we consider the essence of things whether existing or non-existing, we discover that it neither involves existence nor duration, and therefore the essence of existing things cannot be the cause of their existence nor of their duration, but God only is the cause, to whose nature alone existence pertains." This corollary bears a great resemblance to Descartes' argument for determinism and for God's existence. And if we

---

[1] The mystery extends only so far as the "manner" of God's activity, and does not imply that God's omnipotence is suspect. Cf. page 56.

examine it closely it discloses the same ambiguity. For Spinoza is not saying here that without a reference to God a thing may or may not be conceived as existing. The demonstration states only that the existence of anything whose essence does not involve existence cannot be conceived as necessary: "... for (only) that thing whose nature involves existence is the cause of itself and exists from the necessity of its own nature alone."[1] Definition III, Part IV, makes this point clearer. "I call individual things contingent in so far as we discover nothing whilst we attend to their essence alone, which *necessarily* posits their existence or which *necessarily* excludes it." We can only conclude that the existence of individual things is necessitated, or that their non-existence is necessitated, when we understand that they are related in a certain definite manner to God. Again, Axiom I, Part 2, "The essence of man does not involve *necessary* existence; that is to say, the existence as well as the non-existence of this or that man may or may not follow from the order of nature." This does not mean that the existence of this or that man is contingent. It is only so if we attend only to the essence of man. But when we consider that God is the efficient cause of all things (prop. 25) and that "A thing which has been determined to any action was necessarily so determined by God, and that which has not been thus determined by God cannot determine itself to any action" (prop. 26), we can see why the existence of this or that individual thing cannot be regarded as contingent. The first part of proposition 26 asserts that determinism is true, and the second part asserts that freedom is false. And

[1] *Ethics*, demon. prop. 24.

Spinoza finds that the second assertion follows necessarily from the first. "For if a thing which has not been determined by God could determine itself, the first part of the proposition would be false."[1] Proposition 27 states that determination by God involves necessity: "A thing which has been determined by God to any action cannot render itself indeterminate." The proof of this proposition seems to imply that all causes are necessarily connected with their effects and that it is only for this reason that God's determination is necessary. But Spinoza is here trying to demonstrate that there is no contingency in nature. And this cannot be established in terms of an axiom, since, as Hume points out, the statement that every cause necessarily has an effect and that every effect necessarily has a cause establishes nothing but the correlation of the terms cause and effect. It is not a question here as to whether or not "causes" necessarily involve "effects," but as to whether or not any fact necessarily follows from another fact. We may even accept this axiom; but then the question becomes one of discovering whether or not there are any *causes* in nature. Now Spinoza maintains that there is such a cause, namely, God; and from God considered as a cause all effects necessarily follow. Thus proposition 29 contains the desired conclusion. "In nature there is nothing contingent, but all things are determined from the necessity of the divine nature to exist and act in a certain manner."

In considering the succession of propositions from 24 to 29 I have omitted any consideration of proposition 28. I have considered it previously and tried to

[1] *Ethics*, demon. prop. 26.

show that it does not assert the independent existence of a determinate series. It asserts merely that finite things have a certain relation to one another. A finite thing cannot be the cause of the existence or action of another finite thing, unless such a cause be regarded as contingent. That is to say, there is nothing in the nature of any finite thing from which the existence or action of another finite thing necessarily follows. And Spinoza cannot hold that any finite thing is a cause, in the sense of an *originator* of change. The relation between finite things is then, for Spinoza, not any contingent causal relation but a determinate or necessary relation. And in rendering this relation determinate God is not to be considered as the remote cause, as having merely originated the series, but as the immanent cause of each existent and its action. The finite things are involved in what occurs only in the role of occasional causes. "The idea of an individual thing actually existing has God for a cause, not in so far as He is infinite, but in so far as He is considered to be affected by another idea of an individual thing actually existing, of which idea also He is the cause in so far as He is affected by a third, and so on *ad infinitum*."[1] Thus, to say that one individual thing determines another is really to say that God, in so far as He is affected by one individual thing, determines another.[2] If an individual thing or idea is causally related to another individual thing or idea, the connection cannot be considered necessary. But if God is in each case

[1] *Ethics*, Pt. II, prop. 9.
[2] The difficulty of understanding how God can be affected or determined to action by an individual thing will not be discussed here. It appears again more obviously in the writings of Malebranche, and will be treated when we consider them.

the cause, then we have strict determinism or necessary connection.

One final point remains to be considered. It may be said that Spinoza is led to the conclusion that all things are necessary, not because God is the cause of all that occurs, but because "it is not the nature of reason to consider things as contingent but as necessary."[1] If reason must consider all things as necessary, then it matters not what is said about God or anything else. It would be on this view the presupposition of knowledge that no true propositions concerning freedom or contingency are possible. But the demonstration in no way establishes the impossibility of regarding things as contingent, so far as this impossibility is supposed to reside in the nature of reason alone. The demonstration is as follows: "It is in the nature of reason to perceive things truly, that is to say, as they are in themselves, that is to say, not as contingent but as necessary." But it would follow that if things in themselves were contingent, and if it continued to be the nature of reason to consider things truly, then it would be the nature of reason to consider things as contingent. Thus this proposition adds no new arguments for determinism or necessity. There is nothing in reason itself which makes it impossible to assert propositions about contingency or freedom.

I wish now to summarize what has been said and to qualify to some degree an assertion made above. When I said that lacking a reference to God or Substance, Spinoza's statements as to the relations between finite things are meaningless, I meant only that the specification of these relations as necessary depends

[1] *Ethics*, Pt. II, prop. 44.

upon God. I am not denying that many, if not most, of Spinoza's empirical insights into the order of nature and the interdependence of its parts are significant. But there is nothing about any consideration of regularity, order, or dependence which can lead to a categorical denial of the possibility of contingency, freedom, and finite efficacy. Spinoza himself would hold that the mere observation of the order of the world and the relation of its parts led only to truths of the imagination. It is only when through reason we arrive at a knowledge of God's existence and nature that we can comprehend the true relation of all things. And this comprehension discloses that apparent contingency, apparent efficacy, apparent freedom, are in truth only apparent; and that all things are completely determined.

Section 4.—THE ARGUMENT FOR DETERMINISM IN MALEBRANCHE

It seems clearly the case that Malebranche approaches the question of causation and determinism with what is primarily a religious rather than a philosophic interest. "Malebranche . . . wants to demonstrate that God is the sole cause. Occasionalism is not proposed as the solution of a strictly philosophical problem, such as that of the union of the soul and the body. Malebranche examines the notion of cause with a religious interest; and though occasionalism does become one of the principles of his philosophy, Malebranche offers it as a demonstration of the omnipotence of God. . . ."[1] By "omnipotence of God" Malebranche means that

[1] R. Church, *A Study in the Philosophy of Malebranche*, 90.

God is the sole cause of everything that happens, which implies that everything is determined. There is, however, an ambiguity in Mr. Church's statement that Malebranche offers the doctrine of occasionalism as a demonstration of the omnipotence of God; for in terms of the relationships established in Chapter 1 we can fix the direction of the demonstration. I will attempt to show that if Malebranche does succeed in demonstrating anything, he concludes to the truth of occasionalism from the omnipotence of God, and not vice versa. In other words, the alleged fact that finite things are inefficacious is not made the ground for the conclusion that all things are determined (the omnipotence of God), but the alleged fact that all things are determined is made the basis for the conclusion that finite things lack efficacy or cannot be causes. The importance of this question of direction will be made clearer in what follows, but what it involves can perhaps be illustrated if we consider once more the relation of our concepts.

If in any particular case we discover that the proposition "A causes B" is false, it does not follow that A cannot be a cause, or that A is determined. Something else may have caused B and A may have caused C or D. On the other hand, if we know that A is determined, then it follows that any proposition of the form "A causes B, C, or D" must be false. However, if we know that all propositions of the form "A is a cause" are false (that is, that it is false that anything is free), then we likewise know that everything is determined.

If Malebranche's interest, or own own, lay merely in discovering relationships among certain propositions, the direction of the demonstration would be unimportant. But since Malebranche concludes that something is true or false, the direction of his argument is significant. For example, a consideration of matter of fact might convince Malebranche that no finite existents were causes and hence that everything is determined. But statements to the effect that finite things *could* not be causes could only follow from an antecedent decision that all things are determined. The argument might take one of two directions: (1) From the realization that finite existents are never causes to the conclusion that all things are determined, and hence to the conclusion that God is omnipotent; (2) from the realization of God's omnipotence to the conclusion that all things are determined, and hence to the conclusion that finite existents cannot be causes.

Although, as we shall see, Malebranche's argument sometimes seems to develop in the first of these directions, the latter direction represents its true course, since Malebranche never thought it necessary to demonstrate the omnipotence of God. His only concern was to point out that from the truth of God's omnipotence one could conclude that finite existents could not be genuine causes. Hence he considers the supposition that finite existents are causes as "the most dangerous error of pagan philosophy." "But when we come attentively to consider the idea we have of cause or power of acting, we cannot doubt but that it represents something divine: For, the idea of a sovereign power is the idea of a sovereign divinity; and the idea of a subordinate power is the idea of an inferior divinity, yet a true divinity; at least according to the opinion of the heathens supposing it to be the idea of a true power or cause. And therefore we admit something divine in the bodies that surround us when we acknowledge Forms, Faculties, Qualities, Virtues, and all real beings that are capable of producing some effects by the force of their nature; and thus insensibly approve of the heathens, by too great a deference for their philosophy."[1] What Malebranche means in this passage by power is what I mean by cause. And far from being identical with necessary connection (as Hume supposed), so that the denial of power involves the denial of necessary connection, we shall see that it is the assertion of necessary connection or complete determinism made by Malebranche that involves the denial of finite powers. A pagan might assert the existence of such powers; but a Christian, believing firmly in the omnipotence of God, according to Malebranche, would realize that subordinate powers or divinities implied possibilities of actions and results not antecedently determined by God. Since it is blasphemous to question antecedent determination by God, it must be that we deceive ourselves when we assert the existence of finite powers or causes. In short, finite causes are to be denied not because they involve

[1] F. Malebranche, *Search After Truth*, VI, Ch. III, 54. In this passage nothing is implied concerning necessary connection. An inferior divinity might have the power to produce certain effects without supposing that anything necessarily followed from the exercise of such power. There would, of course, be an hypothetical necessity; that is, if a certain effect follows from a certain power or cause and the effect has already occurred, then it is true that it is necessarily false to say that the effect did not occur. If power and effect are regarded as correlative terms, then power necessarily implies an effect. But the point here is whether or not any particular power necessarily results in a particular effect. There may be real beings "capable of producing some effects by the force of their nature" without the slightest evidence for the supposition that from the exercise of power in any particular case a certain particular effect must necessarily follow.

necessity, but because they introduce into the world a measure of contingency not compatible with God's omnipotence. "But that the falsehood of that wretched philosophy[1] and the certainty of our principles and distinctness of our ideas may no longer be doubted, it will be necessary plainly to establish the truths that contradict the errors of the ancient philosophers, or to prove in a few words that there is but one true cause, since there is but one true God; that the nature and force of everything is nothing but the will of God; that all natural things are not real but only occasional causes."[2] Here the direction of the demonstration is obvious: "There is but one true cause (no finite existent can be a cause), since there is but one true omnipotent God."

I wish now to point out what seems to me the exact sense of the opposition between occasional and real causes. Contrary to traditional interpretation, this opposition does not mean the opposition between contingent and necessary succession. I believe this traditional interpretation arises from a confusion in Malebranche—a confusion which was continued and amplified by Hume (cf. Chapter 1). When Malebranche comes to the point of denying finite efficacy, the manifest error of such a denial (and the fact that he elsewhere definitely attributed power to finite existents)[3] leads him to substitute for such a denial the denial of any necessary connection between such finite existents. "But considering our ideas of finite spirits we see no necessary connection betwixt their will and the motion of any body whatsoever; on the contrary,

[1] Any philosophy which supposes that there are finite causes.
[2] F. Malebranche, *Search After Truth*, 55.   [3] Ibid., 3.

we must perceive that there is not nor can be any. Whence we must infer, if we follow light and reason, that as no body can move itself, so no created spirit can be the true and principal cause of its motion."[1] If the doctrine of "occasional causes" is only the doctrine implied by the literal meaning of this passage, the following propositions can be set down as the essence of the doctrine: (1) An occasional cause is one whose connection with its effect is not necessary; (2) an occasional cause may or may not have the *power* to act; (3) God may be or is the only cause from whom certain effects necessarily follow, but God is not the sole active power. But these are not Malebranche's conclusions. In fact, the essence of the doctrine of occasional causes can be stated in three propositions which directly contradict those given above: (1) An occasional cause is one whose connection with its effect is necessary;[2] (2) an occasional cause has no power to act; (3) God is the sole cause or active power.

Malebranche's tendency to use the terms "power" and "necessary connection" interchangeably is perhaps the source of the belief that his argument takes the first direction mentioned above (see page 77); that is, from the assertion that finite existents cannot be real causes (and are occasional causes) to the conclusion that God is the sole real cause. Mr. Church, who accepts this interpretation, adds an observation on

---

[1] F. Malebranche, *Search After Truth*, 55.

[2] Since God is the sole cause and since "we are aware that there is such a connexion betwixt His will and the motion of all bodies, that it is impossible to conceive that He should will that a body be moved, and it should not be moved" it follows that all sequences of events or the relation of occasional causes is necessary. Idem.

Malebranche's conclusion which suggests that Mr. Church has failed to distinguish the idea of necessary connection and the idea of power. "It is equally difficult to find any meaning in the proposition that God is the sole cause. For, in view of the definition Malebranche gives of a cause, we have no more reason to attribute causality to God than to anything finite. . . . Hume urged that divine efficacy is quite as unintelligible as efficacy in finite things."[1] I wish to analyse this statement in order to show that Malebranche did not use one definition of cause but two, and that these two definitions must be distinguished if we are to make sense of Malebranche's argument. For if we chose one or the other exclusively, not only Malebranche's argument but Mr. Church's criticism of it in this statement is invalid. Let us suppose first that Malebranche defined a cause as something necessarily connected with an effect. In terms of this definition the proposition that God is the sole cause is intelligible. To be sure, we may refuse to accept the premise, "God (defined as an omnipotent and omniscient Being) exists"; but if we do, the proposition that God is a real cause (a being from whose will certain effects necessarily follow) definitely has meaning. Further, although Hume denied that we have any impression of divine efficacy, he explicitly asserts that "The order of the universe proves an omnipotent mind; that is, a mind whose will is *constantly attended* with the obedience of every creature and being."[2] He adds that we may know this without it being "necessary we should form a distinct idea of the force and energy

---

[1] R. Church, *A Study in the Philosophy of Malebranche*, 115.
[2] D. Hume, *A Treatise of Human Nature*, 159. Italics Hume's.

of the Supreme Being." Hume can only attest to the fact that the mode of God's action is unintelligible and not that we can give no meaning to the necessary connection between God's willing and the results thereof.

Let us suppose now that Malebranche defined "cause" as power or efficacy, in agreement with the definition given in the opening chapter. It then becomes true to say that "in view of the definition Malebranche gives of a cause" that finite efficacy is quite intelligible. It denotes a fact of immediate experience, an empirical fact.[1] However, any proposition asserting finite efficacy becomes false if we initially accept the proposition that God is the sole cause. If Mr. Church finds it difficult to give this proposition ("God is the sole cause") meaning, he should have no difficulty with the intelligibility of the concept of finite efficacy, or the possible truth of propositions asserting it.

My conclusion is that Malebranche distinguished between necessary connection and power, and that if he seemed to use them interchangeably, it was to lend cogency to the attempted proof that God is the sole cause (in the sense of active agent).[2] The passage in which Malebranche interchanges the terms has been quoted in a previous chapter. I repeat it here for the purpose of illustration: "It is evident, that all bodies, great and little, have no *force* (or power) to move them-

[1] I have not yet examined the perception of causal efficacy. Such an examination is undertaken in a later chapter. It is sufficient to say here that if by cause we do not mean "necessary connection" the idea of cause cannot be disposed of by *a priori* canons of intelligibility.

[2] This interpretation does not validate Mr. Church's criticism of Malebranche's position, since in the statement (quoted on page 81) Mr. Church proceeds on the assumption that Malebranche meant the same thing by power and necessary connection.

selves; a mountain, a house, a stone, a grain of sand, are alike as to that. We have but two sorts of idea, viz. of spirits and bodies; and as we ought not to speak what we conceive not, so must we only argue from these two ideas. Since, therefore, our ideas of bodies convince us that they cannot move themselves, we must conclude that they are moved by spirits. But considering our idea of finite spirits we see no *necessary connection* betwixt their will and the motion of any body whatsoever; on the contrary, we perceive that there is not nor can be any. Whence we must infer, if we will follow the light of reason, that as no body can move itself, so no created spirit can be the true and principal cause of its motion."[1] Malebranche uses the argument in this passage as evidence for the conclusion that God is the sole cause. "But men are so far from being the true causes of the motion produced in their body, that it seems to imply a contradiction that they should be so. For a true cause is that betwixt which and its effect the mind perceives a necessary connection; for so I understand it. But there is none besides the infinitely perfect being, betwixt whose will and the effects the mind can perceive a necessary connection; and therefore none but God is the true cause or has the real power of moving bodies."[2] It seems clear that no action of the will is followed necessarily by the movement of the body, and we may conclude that God is the sole cause, in the sense that He is the one being from whom effects necessarily follow. But Malebranche stretches his conclusion and argues that God is the sole cause in the sense of sole agent. "But when we think of God, or

[1] F. Malebranche, *Search After Truth*, 55.   [2] Ibid., 56.

of a being infinitely perfect, and consequently almighty, we are aware that there is such a connection betwixt His will and the motion of all bodies, that it is impossible to conceive He should will that a body be moved and it should not be moved. And therefore if we speak according to our conceptions and not according to our sensations, we must say that nothing but His will can move bodies. . . ."[1] This is an obvious *non sequitur*. From the statement that God moves bodies, it does not follow that all bodies are moved by God. The conclusion which Malebranche draws would follow only if the premise asserted that it is impossible for a body to move without God willing it to move. But on what grounds could such a premise be established? If we consider "our idea of finite spirits we see no necessary connection betwixt their will and the motion of anybody whatsoever"; but we do not see that it is impossible for any spirit to move a body. And if the proof of God's omnipotence or the fact that He is the sole cause rests upon the assertion that it is impossible for any spirit to move a body, then such a proof has no significance. Since the idea of a finite cause does not involve a contradiction, from the idea alone we cannot conclude that finite causes are impossible or inconceivable. The conclusion follows that Malebranche did not demonstrate the omnipotence of God on the basis of the inconceivability of finite efficacy. But the proposition that God is the sole cause does contradict the assertion that A, B, or C, are causes. Hence we may deduce the impossibility of finite causes from the omnipotence of God.

It follows further that the criterion for the dis-

[1] F. Malebranche, *Search After Truth*, 55.

tinction between occasional and real cause, is not the idea of necessary connection, but the idea of power or efficacy. God is a real cause because He has power to act; finite entities are not real causes, and therefore have no power to act. There is necessary connection between all particulars (occasional causes), but this necessity is not grounded in the particulars themselves, but in the omnipotence of God. This does not mean that we can discover particular cases of necessary connection: "... no necessary connection can be found (in the sense of directly experienced) between the effect and the will of God. All we do know is that God would not be omnipotent if there were any other cause than His will. The conclusion that God alone is the cause rests not on any known necessary connection between His will and any effect we like to imagine, but rather on the idea of the omnipotence of God."[1] The fact that Malebranche can give no account of the manner in which God determines everything that happens does not distinguish him from the other thinkers we have considered. With them also, there was no perception of necessary connection, but only a knowledge of God's omnipotence.

In another passage, Mr. Church states more explicitly the sense in which the denial of finite efficacy is bound up with the assertion of omnipotence: "Thus, the theory of occasional causes virtually gives divine authority to our belief in the uniformity of nature. That uniformity cannot be demonstrated; but once the theory of occasional causes is accepted no demonstration is necessary. We know the divine action is, and is bound to be uniform, and in accord-

[1] R. Church, *A Study in the Philosophy of Malebranche*, 92.

ance to the particular natures of occasional causes. Therefore we know that what is constantly conjoined is connected necessarily."[1] The belief in the uniformity of nature consequent to God's omnipotence, leads to the conclusion that there are no finite causes, no free entities whose activity might upset the order which God has imposed.

The doctrine that God is the sole cause is not the only essential characteristic of occasionalism. The latter doctrine implies also that God is determined by the occasional causes. Mr. Church points out (with Locke) that these two doctrines contradict one another. If God is the sole cause, it cannot be true that anything else influences or causes God to act. In considering the deterministic argument in Spinoza, we came upon a similar difficulty (cf. p. 73). Spinoza holds that: "The idea of an individual thing actually existing has God for a cause, not in so far as He is finite, but in so far as He is considered *to be affected by another idea* of an individual thing actually existing, of which idea He is the cause in so far as He is affected by a third, and so on *ad infinitum*."[2] Now, God cannot be affected by an idea except in so far as He Himself is the cause of that idea, that is to say, He can only affect Himself. What Spinoza requires and what Malebranche attempts to supply with his doctrine of occasional causes is an explanation of the specificity of God's acts. Being "affected by the idea of an individual thing" or being determined by an occasional cause means only that God acts in one way rather than another. But if the occasional cause is nothing

---

[1] R. Church, *A Study in the Philosophy of Malebranche*, 113.
[2] B. Spinoza, *Ethics*, II, prop. 9.

but a particular act of God, then the doctrine that God is determined by an occasional cause becomes meaningless.[1] It is not, however, important for our purposes to consider the merits of the doctrine of occasional causes. If God is the sole cause, then the only thing that can be meant by an occasional cause is a particular act of God. There are other reasons (e.g. the problem of error and evil, reconciling the multiplicity in the world with God's simplicity, etc.) which explain Malebranche's refusal to assert that God indulges in particular acts, and his attempt to explain such acts as due to the determination of God by occasional causes; but these reasons need not concern us, as they have no bearing on our argument.

Section 5.—THE ARGUMENT FOR DETERMINISM IN LEIBNIZ

Before we can decide whether or not Leibniz was a determinist, we must distinguish between the kinds of necessity which he thought could be asserted. He held that not every sense of necessity was opposed to freedom or implied determinism; and he thought that the sense in which what happened in the world was necessary, did not exclude the freedom of finite existents. I shall attempt to show that Leibniz was a determinist despite these qualifications in the same sense as the other philosophers we have examined, and that consequently he denied the freedom of finite existents.

[1] Mr. Church holds that the determination of God by finite causes must have meaning if occasionalism is to mean anything at all. He concludes that such determination has no meaning, and therefore that occasionalism or the term occasional cause has no meaning.

I should say at the outset that my primary concern is not with the question of God's freedom. Leibniz continually confuses or identifies the question of the freedom of finite existents with the freedom of God. The distinction between hypothetical necessity and absolute necessity of which Leibniz makes such frequent use in explaining the sense in which individuals are free, has no meaning when applied to the action of finite existents, and only has meaning in discussing the nature of God. Any discussion concerning the hypothetical or absolute necessity of God's actions turns on the question of the existence of "pure possibles." "If we wish to reject absolutely the pure possibles, contingencies will be destroyed, because if nothing is possible except what God has actually created then what God has actually created would be necessary in case He resolved to create anything."[1] If there are pure possibles then what God created, He created in a free choice. If there are not, then His action in creation must be conceived to be necessary. Since Leibniz believed in the "pure possibles," he regarded what followed in the world consequent to God's choice as hypothetically and not as absolutely necessary. "God is not therefore a necessary agent in producing creatures, since He acts with choice."[2]

Leibniz is constant in his assertion that nothing he has said has in any way impugned God's freedom; and he finds that men misunderstand him on this point because they fail to distinguish hypothetical from absolute necessity. ". . . But it is quite evident that they confuse *necessitatem ex hypothesi* with absolute

---

[1] G. W. von Leibniz, *Correspondence with Arnauld*, 116.
[2] Idem., *Correspondence with Clarke*, 233.

necessity. A distinction has always been made between God's freedom to act absolutely and His obligation to act in virtue of certain resolutions already made."[1] Since I am not concerned with deciding here whether God selects among possibles or acts in the one way possible, I am content for the moment to be included in the "all" of whom Leibniz says that they "agree that God has regulated from all eternity the whole course of the universe without this fact diminishing His freedom in any respect."[2] But does the fact that "God has regulated from all eternity the course of the universe" diminish the freedom of finite existents? It is of no concern to finite creatures whether they

[1] G. W. von Leibniz, *Correspondence with Arnauld*, 77. These antecedent resolutions, however, were made by God and no one else.

[2] Ibid., 78. Absolute necessity may have no meaning when used to describe God's activities even if we deny the existence of the "pure possibles." The existence of the world would still be only hypothetical, the hypothesis being that God had desired to create it. In a letter to Clarke, Leibniz holds that what is really or absolutely necessary is so from its essence alone, since the opposite implies a contradiction. Now if a distinction is made between essence and existence (and this distinction is made by Leibniz), then that which is necessary in terms of its essence is only hypothetically necessary. The opposite of an essence does not imply a contradiction. If it did, then God could not have chosen any other essence than the ones He did choose, since the choice of an opposite essence would have implied a contradiction. "But to say that God can only choose what is best, and to infer from thence that what He does not choose is impossible, this, I say, is confounding terms: 'tis blending power and will, metaphysical necessity and moral necessity, essences and existences. For what is necessary is so by its essence, since the opposite implies a contradiction . . ." (*Correspondence with Clarke*, 161.) It is this last phrase which presents the difficulty. When Leibniz says that what is necessary is so by its essence since the opposite implies a contradiction, the term opposite must refer either to the essence, or the existence, or their relation. It cannot refer to the essence, because the opposite of any essence is possible; it cannot refer to any existent because the opposite of any existent is possible; if it refers, however, to the relation between essence and existence, then it asserts merely a hypothetical necessity. E.g. if it is of the essence of any man to be rational, then any man must be rational. But this is nothing but a statement of hypothetical necessity.

are constrained to act as they do act if they are so constrained, by a necessity of God's nature or by God's free choice. They are concerned not with the origin of the constraint but with its existence; they are concerned to discover whether or not as finite creatures they can cause their own actions even partially. It is obvious that if we take any single event or any single action, we cannot say of that event or action that it is necessary, either absolutely or hypothetically. The necessity of any event can only be asserted as following from something else. Leibniz chooses to call this relation "hypothetical necessity"; and it is important to realize that he did not mean by hypothetical necessity what Dr. Bramhall or Hobbes meant by it. An hypothetical necessity for Bramhall and Hobbes was a necessity of definition, and not an actual necessity. This type of necessity, both Dr. Bramhall and Hobbes agree, cannot be denied. If by hypothesis the entire cause includes the effect, and the entire cause is given, then the effect is necessary. Such a necessity gives no information about matter of fact. But "hypothetical necessity" according to Leibniz involves a *determination* of matter of fact. "Hypothetical necessity is that which the supposition or hypothesis of God's foresight and pre-ordination lays upon future contingencies. And this must needs be admitted unless we deny, as the Socinians do, God's foreknowledge of future contingencies, and His providence which regulates and governs every particular thing."[1] If a conclusion is only necessary in terms of some hypothesis, and we assert the hypothesis, then the conclusion is necessary. It adds nothing to

[1] *Correspondence with Clarke*, 157–9.

say that the necessity is only hypothetical. Since, then, the hypothesis is asserted, namely, that God knows everything antecedently to its occurrence and fore-ordains that occurrence, then what happens is necessary, and the injection of the word "hypothetical" does not qualify this conclusion. Nothing could occur in any other way than it did occur, that is, contrary to God's fore-ordination. To be sure if we take the event by itself, its opposite is not contradictory and might occur. But if we take the event together with the fore-ordination of God (that is, together with the hypothesis) then the opposite of the event is impossible, since it implies the following contradiction: that God determines and does not determine all things. Nor is the distinction between certainty and necessity significant. "To this I reply that a distinction must be made between that which is certain and that which is necessary. Everyone grants that future contingencies are assured since God foresees them, but we do not say just because of that they are necessary."[1] But this is of course precisely what Hobbes says: Everything that happens is necessary because God foreknows what will happen and we cannot, as Leibniz himself says, suppose that God's knowledge has limits or that He may be mistaken, or in short that anything happens which He has not pre-ordained.

I will attempt now to show that the necessity which Leibniz asserts, regardless of the terms he uses in describing it, makes it false to say that individuals or finite existents are free. Leibniz thought that it did not. God may foresee everything, but, according to Leibniz, among other things He may foresee that cer-

[1] *Principles of Metaphysics*, 20.

tain individuals act freely. "I said in the thirteenth article of my summary that the individual concept of each person involves once for all, all that would ever happen to him. From that he draws this conclusion, that all that happens to any person, and even the whole human race, must occur by a necessity more than fatal, as though concepts and previsions rendered things necessary, and as though a free act could not be included in the concept or perfect view which God has of the person who performs it."[1] Of course, if Leibniz means by a free act an act not in itself contradictory, then all acts are free. But is any act free or any event free in the sense in which we have defined freedom? According to our definition, an event is free when activity originates in it. Hence it would be false to say of such an event that it was determined by something else. Since God, for Leibniz, not only foreknows but pre-ordains everything that will happen, no act or event can be free. It is true that Leibniz says that the principles of a monad's actions are contained within the monad, so that what occurs to any individual is not traceable beyond the individual. If this were so, monads would be free, but then it could not be true to say that everything was pre-ordained by God. This opposition can be seen if we examine the test case, as analysed by Leibniz. I contemplate making a journey. Leibniz holds "that I am at liberty either to make or not make the journey, for although it is involved in my concept that I will make it, it is also involved that I will make it freely."[2] Let us suppose that I do not make the journey. If my concept includes everything that happens to me, to say that my concept involves

[1] *Correspondence with Arnauld*, 76. [2] Ibid., 125.

not making the journey "explains" my not making it. But this "explanation" takes no account of God's foreknowledge and pre-ordination. If God, through a complete understanding of my concept, knew in advance (of my decision to go or to stay) that I would go, then the fact that I did not go proves when it occurs that God's foreknowledge is limited and that He may make mistakes. Also, if God had ordained that I should go, and I failed to do so, then God's power would be limited by my free act. In either case it would be false to say that everything is foreknown and pre-ordained by God. "A true providence of God requires a perfect foresight. But then it requires, moreover, not only that He should have foreseen everything, but also that He should have provided for everything beforehand with proper remedies; otherwise, He must be wanting either wisdom to foresee things, or power to provide against them."[1] Here the issue is clearly stated. The hypothesis states that God's foresight and power are perfect, that is, that nothing can happen which He does not know will happen, and that nothing can happen which He has not determined shall happen. Now, to say that God has determined that I shall act freely, is to say no more than that God has determined that I shall act and how I shall act. We cannot assert genuine freedom, or freedom in the defined sense, without denying the hypothesis.

The sense in which Leibniz denied freedom will be more clearly established if we examine his discussion of finite efficacy, since, as we have seen, the truth of determinism implies not only that it is false that any finite entity is free, but that it is false that

[1] *Correspondence with Clarke*, 29–31.

any entity is a cause. The doctrine of the pre-established harmony involves an antecedent determinism and consequently denies the possibility of causal influence. Leibniz states that "The hypothesis of concomitance is a consequence of my notion of substance. For in my view, the individual notion of substance includes all that is ever to happen to it."[1] The fact that the concept of the individual includes all that is ever to happen to the individual "is of great importance and should be firmly established, since from it, it follows that every soul is a world by itself, independent of everything except God."[2] The impossibility of causal efficacy is deduced directly from proposition 13 of the *Discourse on Metaphysics*: "As the individual concept of each person includes once and for all everything which can ever happen to him, in it can be seen *a priori* the evidences or the reasons for the reality of each event and why one happened sooner than the other. But these events, however certain, are nevertheless contingent, being based on the free choice of God and His creatures. It is true that the choices always have their reasons, but they incline to the choices under no compulsion of necessity." We have seen that the "free choice of His creatures" is no choice at all, since God's choice fixes once and for all what can happen to any substance. If what happens to any substance is pre-determined by God, no influence arising in any finite substance can be supposed to interfere with this determination. If one substance could influence another, then from the concept of one individual substance alone, we could not know everything that would happen to it. To say that the concept

[1] *Correspondence with Arnauld* 204. [2] Ibid., 118–19.

of an individual substance includes everything that will happen to the individual is only to say that God in creating any individual pre-ordains everything that will happen to that individual.

The hypothesis of concomitance (pre-established harmony) asserts that the order of nature cannot be understood in terms of the action of finite causes, but only in terms of its determination by God. "This independence (lack of causal relations), however, does not prevent the interactivity of substances among themselves, for, as all created substances are a continual production of the same sovereign Being according to the same designs and express the same universe or the same phenomena, they agree with one another exactly; and this enables us to say that one acts upon the other because one expresses more distinctly than the other the cause or reasons for the changes. . . . It is thus, it seems to me, that the interactivities of created substances among themselves must be understood, and not as though there were a real physical influence or dependence. The latter idea can never be distinctly conceived of."[1] Is it that "physical influence" cannot be conceived because of what has previously been asserted? The absence of causal influence is a postulate of proposition 13, and if we assert proposition 13 then it is true that causal influence is inconceivable.[2] But independently of proposition 13, can it be said that causal influence is inconceivable? Leibniz sometimes says that we are led to the notion of the pre-established harmony, because we cannot explain the relation of substances in terms of causal influence.

---

[1] *Correspondence with Arnauld*, 133–4.
[2] P and not-P cannot both be true.

"But lest those who knew me less should give your words a meaning which we would not like, it will be enough to say that in my opinion it is impossible otherwise to explain transeunt activity (*l'action emanente*) in conformity with the laws of nature, and I thought that the use of my hypothesis would be evident, owing to the difficulty which the most able philosophers of our time have found as to the inter-relation (communication) of minds and bodies, and even of bodily substances with one another: And I do not know but that you yourself have found some difficulty in this."[1] This passage contains many points of great importance. In the first place, Leibniz does not say that transeunt activity cannot be explained without recourse to his hypothesis; he says that transeunt activity is not conformable to the laws of nature. Leibniz is concerned here with the problem that Descartes first perceived: Can minds be supposed to influence bodies and thus upset the laws of nature? The solution is, for Leibniz, that since the laws of nature are nothing but descriptions of God's uniform ways of acting, no influence can be supposed to interfere with such laws and therefore the action of minds upon bodily motions is inconceivable. The pre-established harmony effects this solution by including the action of minds under the laws of nature. That is, minds do not interfere with the movements of bodies, but they appear to, since the same force that determines the movement of the bodies determines the actions of the mind. Minds are included in the system at the price of denying them any genuine causal efficiency. Hence, it is not

---

[1] *The Monadology and Other Philosophical Writings*, tr. by Robert Latta, "Explanation of the new system of communication among substances," 326.

that the inconceivability of causal efficacy leads to the hypothesis of the pre-established harmony; rather, the promise of the infallibility of the laws of nature leads to the pre-established harmony and thus to a denial of causal efficacy. "I reply . . . that this correspondence is of use in explaining the communication of substances and the union of the soul with the body through the laws of nature which have been established *from the first*. . . . For it is to be observed that as there are laws of nature in matter, so there are laws of nature in souls or forms; and the meaning of these laws is that which I have just indicated (pre-established harmony)."[1]

In the second place, the difficulties which arise from attempting to understand the communication of influence between bodily substances, cannot be a genuine difficulty for Leibniz. Matter by definition is incapable of acting and cannot be the cause of anything. Since Leibniz himself denied the existence of anything resembling the Cartesian material substance, the difficulty of understanding how one bit of matter might act on another, should not have led him to assert that causal efficacy is inconceivable. Yet, in another passage he holds more definitely that causal efficacy is unintelligible because the activity of matter is unintelligible: "This vulgar notion in philosophy is not intelligible as the new Cartesians have sufficiently shown. It cannot be explained how immaterial substance is affected by matter. And to maintain an unintelligible notion thereupon is having recourse to

---

[1] *The Monadology and Other Philosophical Writings*, 323. It should be noticed that Leibniz does not think that the laws of nature are derivable from a study of finite causes. Cf. the following chapter, p. 113 *et seq.*

the Scholastic chimerical notion of I know not what inexplicable 'species intentionales' passing from the organs to the soul. Those Cartesians saw the difficulty; but they could not explain it. . . . But I think I have given the true solution (pre-established harmony) of that enigma."[1] In terms of the Cartesian aversion for Scholastic forms, this passage is comprehensible, but Leibniz himself had no such aversion. In his criticism of the Cartesian view of substance, he finds that "the belief in substantial forms has a certain basis in fact, but that these forms effect no changes in the phenomena and must not be employed for the explanation of particular events."[2] Clearly his difficulty here is not with the forms themselves, but with the supposition that such forms have causal influence. Again, "It is true that in my view there are forces (efforts) in all substances; but these forces (efforts) are rightly speaking, only in the substance itself, and what follows from them in other substances takes place in virtue of a harmony pre-established (if I may use the word) and in no wise by any real influence or by the transmission of some species or quality."[3] The forms are unmistakably admitted; but only in order to explain the nature of substance and not to explain causal influences. Leibniz, then, finds no difficulty in the notion of substantial forms; he objects merely to the hypothesis that substances are causally efficacious.

I conclude from the above discussion that Leibniz held the monads to be windowless, since any genuine

---

[1] *Correspondence with Clarke*, 237–9.
[2] *Discourse on Metaphysics*, 15.
[3] *The Monadology and Other Philosophical Writings*, 326.

causal action on the part of the monads would interfere with God's antecedent determinism. That this is the explanation can be finally established, if it is realized (1) that the relation between monads could not be explained in terms of substantial forms or forces, and (2) that even the succession of appetitions or states within the monad could not be explained in terms of the forms. Leibniz says that "these forms effect no change in the phenomena and must not be employed for the explanation of particular events." Particular events are not necessarily cases of interaction; they may be particular acts of any individual monad. It follows that not only the causal independence of monads, but also the causal independence of states within any monad are a consequence of the pre-established harmony or the laws of nature. Hence, when Leibniz says that everything that happens to an individual is traceable to the concept of that individual, he does not mean that the principle of the individual's actions lies within the monad, or that the monad is a cause even so far as its own states are concerned. The individual acts may have their source in the individual concept of the monad, but this means only that they have their source in the antecedent determination by God.

Since the activity of substantial forms is incompatible with the pre-established harmony, we may wonder why Leibniz thought it necessary to "rehabilitate the substantial forms, which are so much decried nowadays." I should suppose that Leibniz saw clearly that substance could not be defined in terms of extension, and that he recognized the significance of Plato's definition of existence (substance) as "power."[1] However, when he turns from a consideration of the nature of individual substances to the consideration of the order of nature, he finds that the individual forces are incompatible with a deterministic world scheme. The deterministic world scheme has its source, not in any consideration of substance, but in the dependence of the world upon God.

Section 7.—SUMMARY

In spite of differences of detail and differences in the manner of statement, the arguments for determinism used by the philosophers we have examined are identical. In no case does the conclusion that all things are determined receive its warrant of authenticity from a concern with empirical fact. All things are determined because, and only because, determinism is implied in the idea of God's omnipotence and omniscience. For the same reason it is false to say that any finite existent is free or is a genuine cause.

This chapter is already too long, and it is unnecessary to say any more about the relation of determinism and causation at this point. In a later chapter I shall show that the attempts to define causation in terms of uniformity originate in the failure to understand this relation.

If the idea of God's omnipotence and omniscience is an immediate intuition, all apparent evidences of causation and freedom must be suspect. An immediate intuition of freedom if joined with the immediate intuition of God's omnipotence and omniscience yields

[1] Leibniz recommended the reading of Plato, especially the *Sophist* in which this definition is found. Cf. Appendix.

the predicament which Descartes realized. For myself, I regard the intuition of freedom as indubitable, and find that the most careful introspection discloses no idea of God's omnipotence and omniscience. This decision is the premise of the arguments for freedom and causation in the following chapters. But it is obvious that the assertion that finite entities are free or causally influence other finite entities cannot be accepted as true by anyone who finds in his experience the intuition which I am rejecting.

CHAPTER III

SCIENCE AND DETERMINISM

THE fact that nothing in the nature of power or causal efficacy involves necessary connection can be seen from the traditional definition of necessity alone. The general definition of necessity current in the seventeenth century was "that the opposite of which is inconceivable." A connection is necessary in this sense when it is inconceivable or contradictory that there shall not be such a connection. It is obvious that no matter of fact relation or connection involves such necessity. It may be true that I have the power to move my body, but there is nothing inconceivable in the idea that after any specific act of willing to move my body, that my body shall not move. This conclusion is a commonplace since Hume. But the important point is that it was a commonplace among the thinkers of the seventeenth century.[1] However, unlike Hume, they did not conclude that therefore there was no necessary connection between finite existents. They secured necessary connection by implicating God in the relations of finite things. If God wills to move a body or if God knows that on such and such a date a body shall move just so much and no farther, it is inconceivable that such an event shall not occur. And if it is inconceivable that an event shall not occur then the occurrence of that event is necessary.

[1] Speaking of the Cartesians, La Forge, Cordemoy, and Malebranche, Mr. Church says, ". . . the one conclusion (the denial of necessary connection) for which Hume is perhaps best known is common to them all." *Hume's Theory of the Understanding*, p. 95.

We have seen that once this conclusion is reached the power or freedom of finite existents also becomes inconceivable. To hold that any entity acts in a manner not determined by God, or in a manner opposed to God's determination, contradicts the idea of God's omniscience and omnipotence, and hence any such action is inconceivable.

Had the assertion of necessity remainded suspended only from the idea of God's omnipotence and omniscience, the denial of this idea or the refusal to consider it as a significant instrument in the analysis of the causal relation, would have opened the way to a more satisfactory account of the causal relation. Subsequent generations of philosophers might have discovered at once the barrier in the way of an understanding of causal efficacy and power. Unfortunately, however, the concept of necessity did not remain so suspended. It was embodied in the structure of seventeenth-century science. There it received the name of scientific determinism and continued to receive assent long after the belief in God's omnipotence and omniscience ceased to be a working hypothesis in science.

Many historians of philosophy have failed to perceive the internal connection between seventeenth-century science and theology. Windelband tells us that the scientific attitude of the seventeenth century involved a "mechanistic despiritualization of nature,"[1] and that "the new methodical principle of mechanics excluded all tracing of corporeal phenomena back to spiritual forces."[2] Undoubtedly there is some justification for this view, as we shall see when we come to investigate the evolution of the concept of matter;

[1] W. Windelband, *History of Philosophy*, 403. [2] Ibid., 401.

but Windelband fails to perceive the distinction that must be made between finite forces, spiritual or otherwise, and the causality of God. The new methodical principle of mechanics implied the tracing of all phenomena back to one spiritual force. This does not mean merely that the seventeenth-century physicists were religious men who added a belief in God as an appendage to their scientific notions. It means that the fundamental scientific notions were little more than statements of God's uniform ways of acting. To be sure, these laws might be discovered through empirical investigation. That is to say, empirical investigation might lead to the discovery of certain uniformities, but these discoveries in themselves could not be made the basis for the assertion of determinism. Determinism is not a corrollary of the idea of "laws of nature," Rather it follows from a certain specific intrepretation of the notion of natural law.[1]

The laws of nature can be regarded as: (1) descriptions of observed phenomena; (2) explanations of observed phenomena; (3) conventional schemes into which we fit our experiences; (4) or as ways of acting imposed by God. No description of observed phenomena legitimately involves the assertion that other relations of phenomena are inconceivable, and that the relations observed are necessary; nor do explanations (however much they may be supposed to differ from "mere" descriptions) legitimately involve necessity. In the attempt to regard laws of nature as conventional schemes, there is an explicit denial of determinism or necessity. It is only if we regard the

[1] For a full discussion of possible interpretations of the notion of "laws of nature" see A. N. Whitehead, *Adventures of Ideas*, Part II, Chap. vii–viii.

laws of nature as imposed by God, that we have any ground for the assertion of determinism. It is inconceivable that a law which God has imposed shall ever be false. To be sure, we may err in our statement or in our understanding of God's laws; and in this sense a discrepancy between the laws and observed phenomena is possible. Nevertheless, if we know that there are such laws, we know that scientific determinism is true, that is to say, that we believe the relations of phenomena to be antecedently necessary. I insert the word antecedently here in order to distinguish the belief in scientific determinism, from the hypothetical necessity or determinism secured through regarding scientific laws as conventional schemes. Such a necessity is an affair of definition alone, and tells us nothing about actual concrete relationships. Undoubtedly, if we eliminate God from questions of physics, such necessity is the only kind that remains; but we cannot avoid the conclusion that the seventeenth century regarded the laws of nature as imposed upon nature by God.

In Mach's *Science of Mechanics* there is an excellent chapter dealing with the infiltration of theological notions into the foundations of mechanics. Mach does not assume that the external opposition of science and theology, and the frequent statements made by men of science that their work was independent of theology, really issued in a divorce between the two. Windelband, for example, takes statements made by Hobbes and Bacon as evidence for the complete disjunction of seventeenth-century science and theology.[1] But Mach's concern with mechanics, rather than with formal pro-

[1] W. Windelband, *History of Philosophy*, 400.

testations of the lack of relationship between science and theology, leads him to the conclusion that mechanics was permeated with theological considerations.[1] More particularly he recognizes that "the notions of the constancy of the quantity of matter, of the constancy of the quantity of motion, of the indestructibility of work or energy, conceptions which completely dominate modern physics, all arose under the influence of theological ideas."[2] From these conceptions it is possible to erect what Mach refers to as a "mechanical mythology." Mach does believe that the content of these laws are empirically significant; it is in the manner in which they were asserted and employed that he finds theological influence. A law may be universally true without in any sense implying the inconceivability of its falsity; the laws become necessarily true only when they are regarded as following, as Descartes thought they followed, from the constancy of God's actions.

So long as it is realized that deterministic physics involves assertions about God, no confusion is apt to arise. But in the case of deterministic physics we have an instance of what I referred to in the previous chapter as a pernicious custom. Long after physicists ceased to base their laws upon considerations of God's modes of acting, they continued to assert the truth of universal determinism. "The French encyclopædists of the eighteenth century imagined they were not far from a final explanation of the world by physical and mechanical principles; Laplace even conceived a mind competent to foretell the progress of nature for all eternity, if but the masses, their positions, and initial

[1] E. Mach, *Science of Mechanics*, 451.   [2] Ibid., 455–6.

velocities were given."[1] Laplace's assertion that he did not need any "hypothesis of the deity" is well known; but he fails to see that without the hypothesis of deity it is nonsense to assert that the progress of nature can be foretold for all eternity. Suppose we imagine a mind competent to know all masses, their positions and their velocities. How from this knowledge could this mind conclude that any future event would necessarily happen? To say that in terms of its knowledge, the laws of nature will enable it to predict with certainty what will happen, does not answer. How can such a mind know that the laws which it knows at any one time will hold in the future? In other words, how is it possible to know that an event in the future must necessarily occur, or that an event might not occur which has not been predicted. There is nothing inconceivable about the occurrence or non-occurrence of any particular event. And Laplace must mean by "foretell" to have certain knowledge of what will occur. For if he means only a probable prediction, then it is unnecessary to have the immense knowledge of all the masses, velocities, and positions. He might have said that any man born on a midnight in July could predict the progress of nature for all eternity. There is nothing inconceivable about such a prediction, and nothing inconceivable about its being true. Laplace, however, did not intend such a trivial assertion. The mind which he imagines must have foreknowledge in the sense in which God is assumed to have foreknowledge; i.e. for such a mind, any mistake is inconceivable and it is inconceivable that nature shall not progress as foreknown. Without

[1] E. Mach, *Science of Mechanics*, 463.

an introduction of a God-like mind, if not God, Laplace can give no meaning to the assertion that it is inconceivable that any event shall or shall not occur; and hence to suppose that physical events are absolutely predetermined without grounding this supposition in the idea of God's activity, is to suppose what is ultimately meaningless.

Once it is recognized that scientific determinism is an embodiment of the idea of God's omnipotence and omniscience, the fact that traditional science has found it impossible to give a satisfactory account of the causal relation becomes entirely understandable. Determinism, in whatever form it is asserted, involves the ultimate incomprehensibility of finite efficacy or the freedom of finite existents. This point is very important. Should the philosopher or man in the street discover that his notions of causation and freedom are opposed by scientific pronouncements, it is probable that he will with too ready humility become suspicious of the deliverances of his own experience, e.g. of his intuition of himself as efficacious. But if he were told that the truth of determinism is not an empirical discovery of science but is rather a disguised reference to the omnipotence and omniscience of God, possibly his eagerness to deny his own experience would be lessened. An example of the opposition between the ordinary notion of causal efficacy and scientific determinism is given by Mr. Eddington. He finds that the "elementary notion of cause and effect is quite inconsistent with a strictly causal scheme (deterministic). How can I *cause* an event in the absolute future, if the future was pre-determined before I was born?"[1]

[1] A. Eddington, *Nature of the Physical World*, 295.

It may be that the determinist can interpret what is meant by my causing any event so that it shall not be inconsistent with determinism; but my point is that there is no need to reformulate our ordinary notions of causation so that they shall be consistent with determinism. The evidence of causal efficacy is evidence that determinism is false; and unless an appeal is made to God's pre-ordination this should be the end of the matter.

Unfortunately, however, this inconsistency between our ordinary notions of causation and determinism was recognized at a period when philosophers and scientists had more respect for the notion of determinism than they have to-day. As a result determinism was retained and the causal relation was redefined. And it is this redefinition that the modern world has inherited as the "regularity view" of causation. I shall return to this question of the development of the regularity view of causation lower down. I wish now to return to the consideration of the influence of determinism upon seventeenth-century doctrines of efficient causation. I shall attempt to show that deterministic physics was not built upon any actual consideration of the causal relation. And that although the scientists and philosophers continued to use the term cause, they had no adequate conception of the causal relation. In other words, although it is true that certain consequences for a doctrine of efficient causation follow from determinism, determinism cannot be derived or deduced from any consideration of efficient causes.

The issue here can perhaps be better understood if we turn to Hume's discussion of efficient causation. Hume assumes that the search for an impression of efficacy is the search for an impression of necessary connection. Since he cannot find any impression of necessary connection, he concludes that there is no impression of efficacy. This procedure would only be justified if it had been the case that previous to Hume an efficient cause had been defined as one necessarily connected with its effect; or if power had been defined as something from which certain specified (in advance) results must necessarily follow. On the basis of such a definition of an efficient cause, coupled with the assertion that nature is nothing but a totality of such causes together with their effects, it is possible to conclude that nature is completely determined. If this were a true statement of the development of determinism, Hume's treatment of the notion of power or efficiency would be significant. However, the statement is not a true description; an efficient cause was not defined as one necessarily connected with its effect and determinism was not deduced from such a definition of efficient causes. In fact the seventeenth century had no adequate doctrine of efficient causes. Hume leads us to believe that this was so because efficient causes were supposed to be necessarily connected with their effects, and thus an empirical instance of such a cause could never be found. This completely reverses the actual situation. The difficulty which the seventeenth-century philosophers and scientists found in the notion of efficient cause was inherent in their recognition that efficient causes operative in nature introduced into nature an element of contingency. They recognized that no deterministic scheme could be erected upon the consideration of such causes. Hence they avoided any clear account of efficient causes, and explained the deterministic scheme as a necessary consequence of God's constant manner of acting. Hume asks the question: "*What is our idea of necessity, when we say that two objects are necessarily connected?*"[1] His answer is that previous philosophers had thought that two objects were necessarily connected when one is the efficient cause of the other. This answer, however, saddles previous philosophers with an absurdity of which they were never guilty. I have been unable to discover any assertion by a first rank thinker of the seventeenth century to the effect that given an efficient cause (finite cause) a specified effect must necessarily follow. When the thinkers of the seventeenth century asserted that objects were necessarily connected they did so quite independently of any concern with the nature of efficient causes, God's causality being excepted.

We cannot justify Hume's mistake on this point by referring to Malebranche's careless usage of the terms "power" and "necessity." The only argument which is not an obvious *non sequitur* for the denial of power in Malebranche depends upon the prior assertion that God is the sole cause, and that things are thus necessarily connected and powerless. Malebranche wished only to show that we could not admit the activity of finite powers without introducing into the world an element of contingency and thus upsetting the omnipotence and omniscience of God. As we shall see, Hume failed to perceive that Malebranche was concerned to establish necessary connection because he had the same unquestioning faith in physical deter-

[1] *Treatise*, I, 153. Italics Hume's.

minism that Malebranche had in God's omnipotence and omniscience.

Some justification for Hume's confusion between necessity and power can perhaps be found in the writings of Hobbes. But, for Hobbes, an efficient cause was not a necessary cause; only the entire cause necessarily involved the effect. Hume realized the circularity of Hobbes' definition of a necessary cause and exposed Hobbes' arguments long before he came to consider the idea of necessary connection.[1] Hobbes does not distinguish between a necessary cause and mere succession in terms of efficiency and power. Hence Hume cannot be referring to Hobbes when he says that power, efficacy, and necessity are synonymous.

In brief, Hume, when he concerns himself with the possible sources of the idea of necessary connection, omits what as a matter of fact was the source of the idea in his predecessors and contemporaries. He says: "Our idea, therefore, of necessity and causation arises entirely from the uniformity observable in operations of nature where similar objects are constantly joined together, and the mind is determined by custom to infer one from the appearance of the other. These two circumstances form the whole of that necessity, which we ascribe to matter. Beyond the constant conjunction of similar objects, and the consequent inference from one to the other, we have no notion of any necessity or connection."[2] I think that I have shown that the real[3] source of the idea of necessary connection is one which Hume does not mention,

---

[1] To be specific, about eighty pages before (Everyman's Edition).
[2] *Enquiry*, 82.
[3] In the sense of "reason" which I have fixed at the beginning of Chapter II. That is, logical source, or ground, or premise.

namely, the idea of God's omnipotence and omniscience. In the *Treatise* Hume does consider the possibility that our idea of *efficacy* is derived from a knowledge of God's efficacy, and he argues rightly that we have no impression of God's efficacy. But none of the men we have considered asserted that they perceived God's efficacy or had an adequate knowledge of the way in which all things followed from His knowledge and will. All that could be known was that if God willed that something should occur, it would be inconceivable that it should not occur; and this for them is a sufficient source of the idea of necessary connection.

In the same sense as the idea of necessary connection does not depend upon any perception of efficacy, the idea of scientific determinism is likewise independent of any perception of efficacy, and arose quite independently of any consideration of the nature of efficient causes. Had the structure of science depended upon an adequate account of efficient causes, we would still be without much of this structure. The very scientists who contributed most to the foundation of modern science expressed a disinclination to concern themselves with this question of efficient causes. Galileo declares, "The present does not seem to be the proper time to investigate the cause of the acceleration of natural motion concerning which various opinions have been expressed by various philosophers, some explaining it by attraction to the centre, others by repulsion between the very small parts of the body, while still others attribute it to a certain stress in the surrounding medium which closes in behind the falling body and drives it from one position to another.

Now, all these fantasies, and others too, ought to be examined, but it is not really worth while. At present it is the purpose of our Author merely to investigate and to demonstrate some of the properties of accelerated motion, whatever the cause of this acceleration might be."[1] The term "present" in this passage refers to the dialogue of the third day. At the conclusion of the third day, Simplicio declares himself convinced by Salviati and asks for information upon this question of causes: "*Simp.*: I am fully satisfied. So now Salviati can explain as promised, the advantage of such a chain, and afterwards present the speculations of our Academician (Galileo) on the subject of impulsive forces (*forza della percossa*); *Salv.*: Let the preceding discussions suffice for to-day; the hour is already late and the time remaining will not permit us to clear up the subjects proposed; we may therefore postpone our meeting until another and more opportune occasion. *Sagr.*: I concur in your opinion, because after various conversations with intimate friends of our Academician I have concluded that this question of impulsive forces is very obscure, and I think that, up to the present, none of those who have treated this subject have been able to clear up its dark corners which lie almost beyond the reach of human imagination."[2] Galileo is here obviously refusing to concern himself with the question of causes. He is content to observe uniformities and deduce other relations from them. But Galileo does not deny the existence of such causes, even in cases where the cause is not perceived. The cause of the acceleration of a falling body is not perceived, but there must be such a cause if the first law

[1] G. Galileo, *Two New Sciences*, 166, 167.   [2] Ibid., 293.

of motion is to be true.[1] It is to be noticed also that for Galileo the notions of uniformity and causation had nothing to do with one another. He recognized that the search for causes was altogether distinct from the search for uniform relationships. Further, in spite of his admitted ignorance upon this question of the nature of causes, he has no hesitation in asserting that man can comprehend the necessary connection of things. "It is true that the divine intellect cognizes the mathematical truths in infinitely greater plenitude than does our own (for God knows them all), but of the few that the human intellect may grasp, I believe that their cognition equals that of the divine intellect as regards objective certainty, since man attains the insight into their necessity, beyond which there can be no higher degree of certainty."[2] It seems to me that this passage, together with the two quoted above, offer conclusive evidence that for Galileo the assertion of necessary connection was not dependent upon any notion of efficiency or causal efficacy.

Newton, like Galileo, evades the question of physical causes. In concluding the eighth definition in the *Principia*, after explaining the relations of forces, he adds: "I likewise call attractions and impulses, in the same sense, accelerative, and motive; and use the words attraction, impulse, propensity of any sort towards a centre, promiscuously, and indifferently, one for another; considering those forces not physically, but mathematically: wherefore the reader is not to imagine by those words I anywhere take upon me

[1] Whether or not we believe the first law of motion is true is not the point. It is undoubtedly the case that Galileo thought it was true.
[2] From *Two Great Systems* quoted from *The Open World* by Hermann Weyl, 10.

to define the kind or the manner of any action, the causes or the physical reason thereof, or that I attribute forces in a *true and physical sense* to certain centres (which are only mathematical points); when at any time I happen to speak of centres as attracting, or as endowed with attractive powers."[1] In the general scholium at the end of the *Principia*, he adds that he has been unable to explain the power of gravity, that is to say, the nature of efficient causes. He suggests that causation involves the action of "a certain most subtle spirit" which lies hid in all things, but he does not amplify his suggestion.[2] The whole structure of the *Principia* is, however, independent of any hypothesis concerning, or description of, physical or efficient causes. When Newton says that gravity exists and acts, he means that particular bodies or spirits exist and act. But knowledge of the uniformity of nature does not depend upon a knowledge of actual efficient causes. He expressed complete ignorance of

---

[1] Sir I. Newton, *Principia*, 5-6. Italics mine.

[2] "Hitherto we have explained the phenomena of the heavens and of our sea by the power of gravity, but have not yet assigned the cause of this power. . . . But hitherto I have not been able to discover the cause of those properties of gravity from phenomena, and I frame no hypothesis; for whatever is not deduced from the phenomena is to be called an hypothesis; and hypotheses, whether metaphysical or physical, whether of occult qualities or mechanical, have no place in experimental philosophy. In this philosophy particular propositions are inferred from phenomena, and afterwards rendered general by induction. . . . And to us it is enough that gravity does really exist, and act according to the laws which we have explained. . . .

"And now we might add something concerning a certain most subtle spirit which pervades and lies hid in all gross bodies by the force and action of which spirit the particles of bodies attract one another at near distances, and cohere, if contiguous; and electric bodies operate to greater distances, as well repelling as attracting the neighbouring corpuscles; and light is emitted, reflected, refracted, inflected, and heats bodies; and all sensation is excited, etc. . . ." *Principia*, III, General Scholium, 546-7.

the nature of the causes of motion. In a letter to Bentley he says: "You sometimes speak of gravity as essential and inherent to matter. Pray, do not ascribe that notion to me; for the cause of gravity is what I do not pretend to know, and therefore would take more time to consider it."[1] In another letter he amplifies his doubts: "It is inconceivable that inanimate brute matter should without the mediation of something else, which is not material, operate upon and affect other matter without mutual contact, as it must be if gravitation, in the sense of Epicurus, be essential and inherent in it. And this is one reason why I desired you would not ascribe innate gravity to me. That gravity should be innate, inherent, and essential to matter so that one body may act upon another at a distance through a vacuum, without the mediation of anything else, by and through which their action and force may be conveyed to one another, is to me so great an absurdity, that I believe no man, who has in philosophical matters a competent faculty of thinking, can ever fall into it. Gravity must be caused by an agent acting constantly according to certain laws; but whether this agent be material or immaterial, I have left to the consideration of my readers."[2] I shall have more to say about the properties of matter in another chapter; but the point here is that Newton confines his interest to the question of uniformity. Ultimately, for Newton, the agent who acts according to constant laws is none other than God.

Newton, himself, makes no assertions to the effect that all things are determined. If we can suppose Clarke to be his spokesman in these matters, he

[1] *Principia*, tr. by Cajori, Appendix, 633. [2] Ibid., 634.

undoubtedly thought that the system of material bodies was a deterministic scheme and reserved freedom for the human soul.[1] This deterministic scheme is not a consequence of any notion of power or efficiency, but is implied in Newton's definition of matter as lacking power or efficiency. With matter defined as dead and inert, both action at a distance and action by contact become incomprehensible. All that can be said is that matter acts according to certain laws. The Cartesians, in spite of their hypothesis of a medium, had no adequate ideas of causal efficacy. Newton's difficulty is not merely a difficulty with the notion of action at a distance; it is a difficulty with the notion of action in general. A deterministic scheme posits the inconceivability of any action. If the word "cause" continues to be used, it must be redefined to express only the regularity of certain sequences. This brings us back to the question of the development of the regularity view of causation.[2]

Let us imagine a closed deterministic scheme consisting of events A, B, C, D, E ... etc. The law which describes the relation of entities in the scheme must be supposed to be necessarily true, so that the failure of any single entity to act in any degree in a manner not prescribed by the law is to be regarded as inconceivable. Granting the existence of such a system, what can be meant by the proposition that C is the cause of D? C by hypothesis is determined, so that it cannot be a cause as I have defined cause. For C to act in a manner not determined by B is inconceivable;

[1] Cf. the Clarke-Leibniz correspondence.
[2] I omit consideration here of the philosophers treated in the preceding chapter. From what was said there it is apparent that for them determinism was not deduced from the nature of efficient causes.

but B cannot be a cause, for B is determined by A. However, unless A is regarded as a cause, we must go outside the system for the entity which determines A. Since by hypothesis, all the entities in the system are determined, the cause of the determination must lie outside the system. Hence the law which states the relations of the entities of the system cannot be derived from a consideration of the system alone. If it is said that the law is nothing but a description of the actual observed relationships of the system, then we cannot speak of the system as a deterministic one, since a description of merely actual relationships observed tells us nothing about unobserved relationships. Suppose we have observed that events A, B, and C are related in a certain manner, and that the statement of this relationship is regarded as the law of the system. There could be nothing inconceivable about such a law being false when it is applied to the relationship of D and E. That is to say, the description of A, B and C tells us nothing about the relations of A, B and C to D and E.

If the assertion "this system is a deterministic system" is to be significant, such an assertion must imply that the law of the system states exactly the relationships of the entities of the system in advance of the occurrence or the observation of such entities; further, this advance statement must not be of the form of a "probable" prediction but of certain knowledge. That is to say, it must be regarded as inconceivable that the law be false. The law of such a system need say nothing about the causal relationships of the entities of the system. It states only that the events in the system follow one another in a prescribed manner, that they *must follow* one another in this prescribed manner. This *must follow* is not derivable from the causal relations of the system, but from the truth of the law of the system.

Coming back, then, to the question asked above; what can be meant by saying that the entities in the system are causally related to one another? According to Eddington such a system is inconsistent with the "elementary notion of cause and effect." And this is so because there cannot be a necessary law of a system of events whose members are genuine causes. This is seen to be the case if we recognize that no law in itself is necessary. There would be nothing inconceivable about a law which stated that bodies attract one another inversely as their mass and directly in proportion to the square of their distance. "Motion itself, and all its quantities and directions, with the laws of gravitation are entirely arbitrary; and might possibly have been altogether different from what they are now. . . . There is not the least appearance of necessity but that all these things might possibly have been infinitely varied from their present constitution."[1] If, however, no law in itself is necessary, what is the significance of the *must follow*? If the laws permit of being infinitely varied, how is it possible to generalize and make assertions about "all bodies" when it is manifest that no one has observed all bodies? The answer to these questions lies in recognizing the relation of the laws to God. The laws themselves do not involve necessity because there is nothing inconceivable about God having chosen other laws. But once God has chosen any law, what happens in the

[1] S. Clarke, *Works*, III, Dem. ix, 42.

world is completely determined according to that law. And this means only that God causes things to happen one way rather than another. Hence, in any genuinely determined system God must be regarded as the cause of all that happens. It follows that no entity in the system can be a cause: A could not cause B, because B is already determined by God. Similarly for all the entities in the system. It is false to say that any entity is a cause of what follows it, because it is true that God determines what follows it. If any entity be a cause, it must be true to say of that entity that some activity originating in it, and not traceable beyond it, influences another entity; but if this is true, it is false to say that God determines whatever happens to the system.

It may be thought that it is possible to avoid this conclusion by redefining causal efficacy, so that the influence of A on B is transmitted by B to C and from C to D, etc. This is the usual manner in which a deterministic scheme is conceived; but it is a view which on analysis exhibits the contradiction which several critics have discerned in the doctrine of occasional causes; "Arnauld insisted rightly that the explanation of the various 'applications' of the will of God by the notion of His being determined by occasional causes, is plausible only if in fact these causes do possess an efficacy of some sort. They must possess not only power to determine God, but also a power to determine themselves; a power to will if the cause be a volition, and a power to produce motion if the cause be a body. . . . The divine volition and the finite volition are not, cannot be, the same, and leave to the term occasional cause any meaning."[1] If, however,

[1] R. Church, *A Study in the Philosophy of Malebranche*, 114.

occasional causes are distinguished from the will of God, it cannot be true that God is the sole cause, and hence it will be false to say that all things are caused by God. This states clearly the difficulty in the notion of the transmission of derived activity or influence. If it is true that B *transmits* activity to C, then it is false that God is the sole cause of what occurs in the system. On the hypothesis that B transmits activity to C, the deterministic scheme is broken down, since it cannot be said that it is necessary that B transmit all the energy it received from A, no more and no less. From a knowledge of the influence transmitted by A to B, it would be impossible to know whether B would influence C in one way rather than another. The determinism can only be restored, if God is considered not only as the initial cause but as the cause of the transmission. This is only repeating what most of the seventeenth-century determinists realized; God must be regarded as the immanent cause and not as a transcendent cause of the happenings in the world. If God is regarded merely as the initial cause, the sequence of events cannot be regarded as necessary; for unless God continually determines the course of nature, the course of nature must be regarded as contingent.

Is it not then clear that the entities which form a deterministic system cannot be regarded as being causally related to one another unless the notion of cause is redefined? But the only relation of such entities compatible with the sole causality of God is the relation of regularity. The entities can be said to succeed one another as God determines them to succeed one another; and since God's action is uniform, the succession of events will be uniform.[1] This, I believe, states the genesis of the "regularity view" of causation. The word "cause" or "action" continued to be used to express the relationship of finite entities, but consistently with the sole causality of God, "cause" or "action" was redefined to mean "follow regularly." This redefinition of causality was current long before Hume analysed the causal situation. Descartes does not state it, but it was implied in his concept of God's continual re-creation. Malebranche's doctrine of occasional causes is ultimately a doctrine that finite entities merely succeed one another and cannot be regarded as causes (as efficacious causes). Leibniz holds that "The action of one finite substance upon another consists only in the increase in the degrees of expression of the first combined with a decrease in that of the second, in so far as God has in advance fashioned them so that they shall act in accord."[2] This is manifestly a statement of the uniformity view of causation. And although the word action is used and redefined, it is obvious that Leibniz is here denying the causal action of one substance upon another.

In itself "a regularity view" of causation does not imply the denial of causal efficacy. There are degrees of uniformity; and there is nothing in the notion of uniformity which makes freedom or causal efficacy inconceivable. But uniformity is compatible with strict determinism and freedom and causal efficacy are not.

[1] "We also know that there is perfection in God, not only because He is in Himself immutable, but because He operates in the most constant immutable manner possible." R. Descartes, *Works*, I, *Principles*, Pt. 2, princ. 36.

[2] Leibniz, *The Monadology and Other Philosophical Writings*, 26.

So long, however, as the concept of "uniformity" really means absolute uniformity or determinism, the notion of causal efficacy is excluded. And it is because Hume thought of uniformities as absolute that he could give no satisfactory account of causal efficacy. "He thought of cause in terms of experimental science, that is to say, as consisting of supposedly invincible uniformities, and therefore he did not even contemplate the possibility of non-uniform causes."[1] However important the doctrine of invincible uniformities may have been to the science of Hume's day, the notion of uniformity neither implies nor excludes the concept of efficacy. There is, of course, no grave philosophic error involved in redefining words. If scientists wish to use the word "cause" when what they mean is "uniformity," any serious protest is so far absurd. However, if such a redefinition obscures the fact that the term "cause" originally had an ostensive definition a protest is so far in order. For if the term is used in its original sense as describing a certain matter-of-fact relation between events, a problem is created if he who has so used the term is told that all he could mean is that one event follows the other uniformly. The fact which the user of the term may wish to describe may have nothing at all to do with uniformity.

Hume's confusion of "necessary connection" with "power" leads him to deny that we experience "power." Locke had stated that the idea of power or efficacy was a simple idea derived from reflection upon the operation of our own minds. Hume sets himself to examine this notion. "We shall proceed to examine

[1] J. Laird, *Hume's Philosophy of Human Nature*, 103.

this pretension; and first with regard to the influence of volition over the organs of the body. This influence, we may observe, is a fact, which like all other natural events, can only be known by experience, and can never be foreseen from any apparent energy or power in the cause, which connects it with the effect, and renders one an infallible consequence of the other."[1] It is clear that if the investigation concerns efficacy, Hume has admitted that we do perceive such efficacy. ("This influence, we may observe, is a fact, which like all other natural events, can only be known by experience.") But what need is there to go on; neither Locke nor anyone else supposed that we perceived an *infallible* influence. The perception of power is altogether distinct from the question of infallible or necessary connections.

I do not think that Hume's confusion of these two concepts is explicable solely by reference to the similar confusion in Malebranche. A more probable reason is that Hume was not interested in the question of the causal relation at all. He was instead interested in the question of determinism. That is, the purpose of his investigation was not to discover the nature of the causal relation, but to discover whether the truth of determinism can be demonstrated or must be accepted on faith. Hence he questions the avowed perception of efficacy that he might discover whether such a perception could be made the grounds for the assertion of necessary connection or complete determinism. The conclusion that it can not is obvious from the definition of necessary connection alone. Hume, however, was not content to recognize this fact; since

[1] Hume, *An Enquiry Concerning Human Understanding*, 65.

necessary connection cannot be grounded in the perception of efficacy, he continues to search elsewhere for the ground of necessary connection. He finds only a tendency of the human mind to regard things as necessarily connected, a tendency which was later stepped up by Kant to the status of a category.[1]

The assertion of "regular sequence" is nothing but the assertion of determinism with its teeth drawn. The assertion of determinism implies that events follow one another in certain ways specifiable and knowable in advance, that is to say, regularly; and from this notion the redefinition of the causal relation follows as a matter of course. Since the term causation is used to denote a matter-of-fact relationship between two existents, it comes to mean that one existent follows regularly from the other. It should be clear that this phrase "follow regularly" says nothing about causation at all and is really the assertion of necessary connection disguised as scientific determinism.

This last can perhaps be seen more clearly if we consider any two events said to be causally connected. The proposition "A causes B" describes an actual relationship between two events. This relationship is not identical with the relationship of succession. It may be true that "A is followed by B" and false that "A causes B." The rising of the sun may follow the crowing of the cock, but it does not follow that the crowing is the cause of the sun's rising. If the phrase "follow regularly" is substituted for "follow" we can no longer be understood as describing a matter-of-fact

[1] I shall return in a later chapter to a more detailed exposition of this interpretation of Hume and Kant, since it is usually supposed that because Hume and Kant continued to use the word cause, that they were actually talking about an actual relationship of finite existents.

relation between two events.[1] There can be no empirical difference denoted by the propositions "A follows B" and "A regularly follows B," so far as the relationship of A and B are concerned. The proposition "A regularly follows B" means only that "A follows B" and that if B could be repeated A would follow it again. It is dubious, of course, whether or not any event is ever repeated, so that the "regularity view" cannot be stated "same cause, same effect," but only as "if the same cause is given, the same effect will follow." Stated in this way, it is obvious that the "regularity view" is not a description of any actual relationship between events, but the assertion that the sequence of events is necessary. If we know that the same cause is always followed by the same effect, then we know that all things are necessarily connected. Even if it is said with Hume that we only believe that the same cause will have the same effect, this can only mean that we believe that things are necessarily connected.

The question of the nature of causation is not answered by the expression "same cause, same effect"; for such a phrase tells us nothing about the relationship of cause and effect, except that the events which we designate as cause and effect are necessarily connected. What we wish to know is whether or not there is any empirical difference in the relationship of two events expressed by the propositions "A is caused by B" and "A follows B." The "regularity view" unless it wishes to add the assertion of necessary connection, states that the empirical fact described by both propositions is identical. Now this is more than a redefinition of terms. So long as the regularity

[1] There is no denotable relation of "regular succession."

view follows from a prior determinism, it can make a distinction between the terms follow and cause, independently of any empirical concern with the actual relationship of events. If, however, the determinism is discarded, the regularity view can only be defended on the ground that as a matter of fact all that is ever perceived, so far as the relationship of events is concerned, is the relationship of succession. This last assertion, viz. that "all that is ever perceived is the relationship of succession" is, I hope to show, manifestly false. It is currently regarded as indubitable because it is thought that the alternative is the assertion of the perception of necessary connection. But, as I have attempted to prove, there is no reason, historical or otherwise, to regard the perception of necessary connection as the alternative; before Hume, the philosophers of the seventeenth century clearly realized that no perception *could* disclose any necessary connection between distinct events. Hence the legitimate alternative to the proposition "all that is ever perceived is succession" is the proposition which asserts that causal influence is perceived. That such influence is perceived is, of course, the presupposition of an ostensive definition of causation. Hume is correct when he argues that "should any one . . . pretend to define a cause by saying it is something productive of another, it is evident he would be saying nothing. For what does he mean by production? Can he give any definition of it, that will not be the same with that of causation? If he can, I desire it may be produced. If he cannot, he here runs in a circle, and gives a synonymous term instead of a definition."[1] By the

[1] *Treatise*, I, 80.

same argument anyone asserting that to succeed means to follow would be open to the accusation of running in a circle and consequent meaninglessness. If one might ask Hume what he meant by succession, would he not reply that a definition was impossible and that he could only point to some actual experience to which we could apply the term succession? The same answer can, however, be given in reference to causation. In order to know what causation means, we can only designate the empirical situation which gives the term its meaning. This is obviously what Locke meant when he called power a simple idea.

Ostensive definition does not establish any necessary connection between a term and what it denotes. It is always possible to use the term to denote a completely different fact. Hence, if one wishes to use the term "cause," as a synonym for the term follow, nothing more disastrous would occur than that in the interest of clarity we should use another term for what was originally denoted by the term cause. If, however, the use of the terms "cause" and "follow" as synonyms involves the assertion that nothing is ever perceived but the relation of succession or "following," it ceases to be a question of word usage and becomes a question of fact. Concerning questions of fact, no definitions are required. It is only necessary to examine one's experience to discover whether or not there is any perceived difference between the relation of succession and the relation of causation.

I

CHAPTER IV

HUME'S SCEPTICISM IN ITS RELATION TO CAUSATION AND DETERMINISM

By the time Hume wrote his *Treatise* the concept of universal determinism had become an integral part of scientific thought. Hume perceived that most men accepted this concept without inquiring into its origin and validity. Thus, his self-imposed task was the discovery of the source of this belief in universal determinism and the defence of the belief against those who supposed it false. Hume engaged in what is usually called rationalization, and searched for arguments to substantiate a conclusion which he did not doubt. Concerning this conclusion, Hume is never sceptical. His scepticism extends only so far as what he regarded as the usual arguments for the conclusion. Positive arguments against the conclusion which have their origin in the experience of freedom, the experience of irregularities in nature, or the belief in miracles he dismisses by appealing to the undoubted truth of the conclusion. His procedure is circular; he can find no arguments for the conclusion that everything is determined, yet he refuses to accept the deliverances of experience and the testimony of others on the ground that everything *is* determined. After avowedly showing that we have no warrant from reason or experience for the belief in necessary connection, when he comes to consider the question of human freedom, he argues that "It is universally acknowledged that the operations of external bodies are necessary and that, in the communication of their motion, in their attraction, and mutual cohesion, there are not the least traces of indifference or liberty. Every object is determined by an absolute fate to a certain degree and direction of its motion, and can no more depart from that precise line in which it moves, than it can convert itself into an angel, or spirit or any other superior substance."[1] And he attempts to show that the actions of men are alike necessary. To be sure, he qualifies his argument with the statement that the necessity he asserts is nothing more than constant union and the inference of the mind. "I can imagine only one way of eluding this argument, which is by denying that uniformity of human actions, on which it is founded."[2] Here the term "uniformity" lends an ambiguous plausibility to Hume's argument. Uniformity is a matter of degree; no one would deny that men's actions are uniform to a degree. But similarly no one would (or should) deny that men's actions exhibit a degree of irregularity. No "Newton" had as yet appeared to predict the exact actions of a man from the consideration of his motives. When the term "uniformity" is referred to bodies it does not mean more or less uniform but absolutely uniform. ("Every object is determined by an absolute fate to a certain degree and direction of its motion, and can no more depart from that precise line in which it moves, than it can convert itself into an angel or spirit. . . .") But no one in Hume's time or since has had any evidence to believe that given a man's motives on one day, it would be possible to predict absolutely that two days hence he would kill a man by stabbing a knife into the man's abdominal region; and that the

[1] *Treatise*, II, 113-14.   [2] Ibid., 116.

knife would enter to the depth of 4·189 inches and pierce the skin just twelve inches from the chin on a right line drawn from the tip of the nose to the crotch. If such a prediction is not possible, what is meant by the uniformity of men's actions? Hume cannot argue that "if we knew the hidden causes" we could predict with the required degree of accuracy, because his argument is, he tells us, based only upon the *actual* perception of uniformities.

If by the uniformity of human actions Hume means only the degree of uniformity observed, then he must also allow the degree of irregularity observed. It may be true that most men with murderous impulses become murderers, but it is likewise true that some men with murderous impulses do not become murderers. Hume, as we should expect, recognizes this fact: "Now, some may perhaps find a pretext to deny this regular union and connection. For what is more capricious than human actions? And what creature departs more widely, not only from right reason, but from his own character and disposition?"[1] But, he argues, the cases of apparent (experienced) irregularity are no more serious than experienced irregularities in the relation of bodies. We do not accept the irregularities of bodily motions as overthrowing physical determinism and necessity; hence there is no reason to regard the inconstancy of human actions as overthrowing moral necessity. It is only necessary to recognize, according to Hume, that an underlying uniformity is to be found in all human activity and that without the belief in such uniformity society could not continue. "A merchant looks for fidelity and skill in his factor or super-

[1] *Treatise*, II, 116.

cargo. A man who gives orders for his dinner doubts not of the obedience of his servants. . . . Now I assert that whoever reasons after this manner, does, *ipso facto*, believe the actions of the will to arise from necessity, and that he knows not what he means when he denies it."[1] But surely this is an extreme conclusion on such slender evidence. The same merchant may bond his supercargo, and the same man may be forced to discharge a servant who is disobedient. The merchant who bonds his supercargo not only does not believe that because a man has been honest in the past that he will be honest in the future, and that such a man's actions follow uniformly from his character; on the contrary, he has a positive belief that the actions of men are not uniform. When the merchant bonds his supercargo he not only denies necessity in Hume's sense, but he knows what he means when he denies it. If the *fact* of belief in the uniformity of men's actions implies the belief in necessity, then the fact of disappointment proves that men's actions are not necessitated. It may be the case, as Hume argues, that "Motion in one body, in all past instances that have fallen under our observation, is followed upon impulses by motion in another."[2] Perhaps no one has ever been disappointed in expecting a body to move or the sun to rise. But most certainly men have misplaced their trust and have been disappointed in friendship and love; and having been so disappointed, on Hume's own grounds there remains not the slightest basis for the belief that "actions of will rise from necessity."

Ultimately Hume has no other basis for the denial

[1] *Treatise*, II, 118. [2] Ibid., 119.

of human freedom than a dogmatic (non-empirical) belief that all things are determined. There is nothing more sacrosanct in the observation of constant conjunction and the inference of necessity, than there is in the observation of irregularity and the inference of freedom. If, as Hume says, there "are two particulars which we are to consider as essential to necessity, viz. the constant union and the inference of the mind; and wherever we discover these, we must acknowledge a necessity";[1] it follows that in the absence of such observation and in the absence of such an inference, necessity is also absent. Now men do not observe a constant union in human actions, *nor do they as a matter of fact always infer that such actions are necessary*. In other words, the very supposition of freedom is sufficient to abolish necessity. If there is no tendency of the mind to regard things as necessarily connected, then according to Hume no meaning can be given to the concept of necessary connection. Hence, when a man discovers no such tendency and rather discovers a tendency to regard things as free, it becomes meaningless to assert that nevertheless they are necessary.

It seems to me clear that Hume denies human freedom, not because investigation discloses that human actions are necessary but because he approaches the investigation of the question with a prior assurance that all things are necessary. He refuses to place his trust in actual experience, and dismisses the experience of liberty as *"a false sensation or experience"* (italics Hume's). He says: "We may imagine we feel a liberty within ourselves, but a spectator can commonly infer our actions from our motives and character; and even

[1] *Treatise*, I, 114.

where he cannot, he concludes in general that he might, were he perfectly acquainted with every circumstance of our situation and temper, and the most secret springs of our complexion and disposition. Now this is the very essence of necessity according to the foregoing doctrine."[1] But does not this question remain: in the case where the spectator cannot infer our actions, how can he know that even if he knew all the causes he could infer our actions? Of course, if all the relevant causes included the effects, no inference would be needed; but for Hume the essence of necessity involves an actual inference. He means by necessary connection that given all the causes, we can infer with certainty all the effects.

What now can be said concerning Hume's "prodigious discovery concerning causes?" The necessity he asserts is the same necessity which was asserted by Leibniz, by Descartes, and by Malebranche. The elimination of *efficacy* from the relationships of finite existents does not distinguish Hume's conclusions; Leibniz, Descartes, and Malebranche all deny the efficacy of finite existents. To be sure these last three, Descartes, Leibniz, and Malebranche, based their assertions of necessary connection upon the prior belief in God's uniform ways of acting; but this only serves to distinguish them from Hume as being more acute. Hume has given us no reason for concluding that in every case, given the cause, it is possible to infer the effect; that is to say, his necessity is dogmatic and uncritical. This unquestioned belief in the truth of determinism underlies Hume's entire discussion of the causal relation; he approaches the question of the

[1] *Treatise*, II, 121.

nature of causation not directly to discover what the nature of causation may be, but to discover whether or not there is anything in actual perceived relations which justifies the belief in determinism. He dismisses efficacy, not because such efficacy is unperceived, but because its perception cannot be made the basis for the assertion of necessary connection. This means that for those who are concerned with the nature of the causal relation and not with the question of necessary connection or determinism, Hume's conclusions concerning the causal relation are simply not to the point. It is to no purpose to say that Hume defined the causal relation as a case of necessary connection; because, according to Hume's own arguments, this would mean that causation (i.e. necessary connection) is not a matter-of-fact relation.[1] It would remain necessary for those interested to investigate empirically the actual relationship of finite existents. Hume holds that even though we cannot demonstrate, nor intuit, nor empirically verify our belief in necessary connection, nevertheless we must continue to hold to the belief. And this "must" cannot be reduced to a tendency of the human mind; for the very existence of the question of freedom is evidence that this "must" is not a universal tendency, and that some minds feel a tendency to deny necessity and assert freedom. The fact that Hume refused to accept this result seems to me to be conclusive evidence that, although Hume could find no grounds empirical or rational for his belief in necessary connection, he continued to hold the belief and insisted that others should hold it.

It may be said that Hume's discussion of human

[1] See below.

freedom is merely an unfortunate appendage to his more serious concern with the question of causation. Hence I shall undertake to show that throughout Hume's entire argument the belief in determinism or necessary connection remains unquestioned, and that his treatment of the actual nature of the causal relation is thereby prejudiced. All of his arguments are directed to this one question: What reason have we for believing that things are necessarily connected? I have shown that Hume's predecessors never supposed that the answer to this question could be found in any consideration of the nature of the causal relation. Hume's confusion between the two questions, the question of determinism and the nature of the causal relation, has been transmitted to modern philosophy through Kant. Kant's category of causality says nothing at all about the nature of the causal relation, but only that Hume's tendency to regard things as necessarily connected must be a category of the human mind. It is the confusion between "determinism" and "causation" which makes most modern discussions of the causal relation so unsatisfactory. The discussions shift back and forth from discussions of determinism to empirical assertions as to what is actually perceived; but questions of determinism are not and cannot be empirical questions, and questions as to the perceived relations of existents cannot be intelligently converted into questions as to the truth or falsity of determinism. The importance of this point justifies a thorough analysis of Hume's arguments, even though Hume's writings fall outside the period with which I have been mainly concerned.

Hume's confusion between determinism and causation is apparent in his initial statement of the question. The only relation ". . . that can be traced beyond our senses, and informs us of existences and objects which we do not see or feel is *causation*."[1] Is this not a description of what is implied by the truth of determinism rather than a description of a matter-of-fact or empirical relation? Hume uses the term "causation"; but he does not use it to describe some observed relationship but as involving the possibility of inference. Hence, Hume holds that the relation of "causation" involves not only priority and contiguity but necessary connection. "An object may be contiguous and prior to another, without being considered its cause. There is a necessary connection to be taken into consideration; and that relation *is of much greater importance* than any of the other two mentioned above."[2] Here we see plainly that Hume's interest lies not in discovering the nature of any empirical relation, but in discovering why the causal relation is taken to involve necessary connection. That it was so taken, he never doubts. That it was not so taken, I have been concerned to point out. Hume to be accurate should have said: *I* suppose the relation of causation to involve necessary connection, and *I* am going to search for the origin of *my* idea.

When Hume examines the relations of objects he declares that he "can find none but those of contiguity and succession."[3] Now this statement is, I think, false, and Hume afterwards admits its falsity; but its truth or falsity is not important at this point. Whatever other relation is observed, there can be no doubt

---

[1] *Treatise*, I, 78. Italics Hume's.
[2] Ibid., 80. Italics mine.
[3] Ibid., 80.

that the relation of necessary connection will not be observed. Since this relation cannot be observed, and since it is regarded by Hume as the most important element of the causal relation, he proposes to "beat about all the neighbouring fields" in the hope of discovering its origin.

Had Hume really been interested in discovering the nature of the causal relation, he could have avoided this excursion into neighbouring fields. Since causation is a matter-of-fact relation, it is only necessary to observe matter-of-fact relations, and to discover the one which we call the causal relation. I have previously quoted the passage in which Hume objects to the attempt to define causation in terms of production. But Hume should have realized that no matter-of-fact relation can be defined; it must be experienced (and defined ostensively). For example, Locke does not attempt a definition of power; he searches his experience for the fact designated by the term.

Hume, however, does recognize that no experience discloses necessary connection and hence that necessary connection is not a matter-of-fact relation. Consequently, his search through the neighbouring fields is not an empirical investigation into the nature of a matter-of-fact relation, but a search for the origin of a belief. A contradiction is implied here which Hume must have seen had he been genuinely interested in the causal relation rather than in the question of determinism. Initially he declares that causation is a matter-of-fact relation. Secondly, he states that necessary connection is the most important element in the causal relation; and thirdly, that no distinct objects can be necessarily connected. These three assertions cannot all be true, yet all are essential in Hume's argument. It is no wonder that Hume finds himself driven to scepticism in his analysis of causation. He has failed to distinguish causation from determinism; the former is a matter-of-fact relation; the latter implies necessary connection, and is not a matter-of-fact relation.

The search through the neighbouring fields begins with an examination of two questions: "First, for what reason we pronounce it necessary, that everything whose existence has a beginning, should also have a cause? Secondly, why we conclude that such causes must necessarily have such particular effects; and what is the nature of that *inference* we draw from one to the other, and the *belief* we repose in it?"[1] Hume does not deny that everything which has a beginning has a cause; he maintains merely that the truth of this proposition can neither be demonstrated nor intuited. "Allow me to tell you that I never asserted so absurd a proposition as that anything might arise without a cause. I only maintained that our certainty of the falsehood of that proposition proceeded neither from demonstration nor intuition, but from another source. That Cæsar existed, that there is such an island as Sicily—for these propositions, I affirm, we have no demonstrative proof—would you infer that I deny their truth, or even their certainty? There are many different kinds of certainty; and some of them as satisfactory to the mind, though perhaps not so regular, as the demonstrative kind."[2]

There is a sense (though perhaps an unimportant

[1] *Treatise*, I, 81. Italics Hume's.
[2] Letter, quoted from J. Laird, *Hume's Philosophy of Human Nature*, 96.

sense) in which the proposition "whatever begins to exist must have a cause of existence" is demonstrable. If the phrase "begins to exist" means "is produced," the proposition is capable of demonstration since it becomes tautologous: "Whatever is produced must have a cause (a producer) of existence." However, Hume holds that the idea of "beginning to exist" and the idea of production are distinct and separable,[1] and hence that the proposition cannot be demonstrated. This reasoning is unanswerable; but its further use to show that the arguments of Hume's predecessors were "fallacious and sophistical" is questionable. Locke's assertion that the very idea of production makes it absurd to suppose that nothing could produce anything is undoubtedly analytic and therein lies its strength. Hume, in answering Locke, holds, "It is sufficient only to observe, that when we exclude all causes we really do exclude them, and neither suppose nothing nor the object itself to be the cause of the existence; and consequently can draw no argument from the absurdity of these suppositions to prove the absurdity of that exclusion. If everything must have a cause, it follows that, upon the exclusion of other causes, we must accept the object itself or nothing as causes. But it is the very point in question, whether everything must have a cause or not."[2] If this is the point in question, then it is not what I take Locke's point to be. Locke does not say that everything must have a cause;[3] he says only that that which is caused or produced must have a cause. Hume, however, supposes that he has refuted Locke[4] and goes on to

---

[1] *Treatise*, I, 82.   [2] Ibid., 84.
[3] J. Laird, *Hume's Philosophy of Human Nature*, 99.   [4] *Treatise*, I, 84.

say that "it is not from knowledge or any scientific reasoning, that we derive the opinion of the necessity of a cause to every new production...."[1] He fails to see that since the idea of production implies the idea of a cause, by definition every new production must have a cause, and that the proposition is thus demonstrable. However, what Hume undoubtedly means is that the idea of "beginning to exist" is distinct from the idea of "production or cause"; hence, their connection is not demonstrable. Whether or not they are distinct need not concern us. The important point is that if Hume's predecessors were "sophistical" for treating the ideas as identical and basing a demonstration upon this identity, by the same reasoning, Hume's argument is sophistical, for he first posits the ideas as distinct and then argues that no demonstration of their identity is possible.

Hume does not conclude that our belief that "whatsoever begins to exist must have a cause of existence" is false. Rather, having decided that the truth of the belief cannot be demonstrated, he asks "how experience gives rise to such a principle."[2] The answer to this question is not given directly. Hume thinks that "it will be more convenient to sink this question in the following, *why we conclude, that such particular causes must necessarily have such particular effects, and why we form an inference from one to another?*"[3] This "sinking" of the general question bears out what has been suggested above, namely, that the question is merely verbal. The necessity of a cause to every beginning is not a question of necessary connection, but a question of the meaning of the word "beginning."

[1] *Treatise*, I, 84.   [2] Ibid., 84–5.   [3] Ibid., 85. Italics Hume's

But the concept of necessary connection is directly involved in the second question. For this reason, Hume should not have used the royal "we." All men do not conclude that particular causes must necessarily have certain particular effects. Hume should have asked, "why *I* conclude, that such particular causes must necessarily have such particular effects, etc. . . ." It is only on the assumption that this belief is universal, however, that Hume's investigation has genuine importance. For this reason Kant's conclusion that the belief has its roots in a category of the human mind represents a significant advance in the development of this doctrine.

Continuing his argument Hume holds that the inference from cause to effect cannot be an affair of reason or knowledge since the non-occurrence of the particular effect in any given case does not imply a contradiction: "Such an inference would amount to knowledge, and would imply the absolute contradiction and impossibility of conceiving anything different. But as all distinct ideas are separable (the idea of the cause and the idea of the effect) it is evident there can be no impossibility of that kind."[1] The causal inference, then, must be based on experience. "The nature of experience is this. We remember to have had frequent instances of the existence of one species of objects; and also remember, that the individuals of another species of objects have always attended them, and have existed in regular order of contiguity and succession with regard to them. Thus, we remember to have seen that species of object we call flame, and to have felt that species of sensation

[1] *Treatise*, I, 89.

we call heat. We likewise call to mind their constant conjunction in all past instances. Without any further ceremony, we call the one the cause, and the other effect, and infer the existence of the one from the other. . . . Thus in advancing we have insensibly discovered a new relation betwixt cause and effect when we least expected it, and were entirely employed on another subject. This relation is their constant conjunction."[1]

But how does this "new relation" help us to find the nature of the causal inference? There can be no demonstrative argument to the effect "that those instances of which we have had no experience resemble those of which we have had experience."[2] Further, Hume holds that there can be no basis for any probability judgment about the unexperienced cases; for such judgments are founded upon the presumption of a resemblance of experienced and unexperienced instances, and cannot be made the basis for the presumption.

Hume next considers whether or not the question is illuminated by the introduction of the idea of power or production. (His more detailed discussion of power is reserved for a later chapter.) "It shall therefore be allowed for a moment, that the production of one object by another in any one instance implies a power; and that this power is connected with its effect. But it having been already proved, that the power lies not in the sensible qualities of the cause; and there being nothing but the sensible qualities present to us; I

---

[1] *Treatise*, I, 89–90. This last statement is careless. There is obviously no discovery of a new relation; there is only a multitude of experiences of the same relation.   [2] Ibid., 91.

ask, why in other instances you presume that the same power still exists, merely upon the appearance of these qualities? Your appeal to past experience decides nothing in the present case; and at the utmost can only prove that that very object, which produced any other, was at that very instant endowed with such a power; but can never prove that the same power must continue in the same object or collection of sensible qualities; much less that a like power is always conjoined with like sensible qualities. Should it be said, that we have experience, that the same power continues united with the same object, and that like objects are endowed with like powers, I would renew my question, *why from this experience we form any conclusion beyond those past instances, of which we have had experience?*"[1]

This passage presents several curious statements and difficulties. In the first place, Hume is really allowing nothing when he "allows that the production of one object by another in any one instance implies a power"; any actual production of one object by another implies by definition a "power" in the producing object. Otherwise it is difficult to see what can be meant by either power or production. In the second place, Hume asserts that it has "already been proved that power lies not in the sensible qualities of the cause." Now this is either a definition of what Hume chooses to call "sensible qualities" or it is nonsense. If "sensible quality" is a class name for those things actually experienced, that is, for matter of fact, any question of proof or demonstration concerning the existence of a sensible quality or the

[1] *Treatise*, I, 93. Italics Hume's.

fact that it is experienced is meaningless. Since the existence or non-existence of any matter of fact is always conceivable, it is impossible to prove that power as a character of matter of fact does not exist. Hume can mean only that in the inventory of those things which he experiences he discovers nothing which is or resembles what men normally call power. This is an autobiographical detail and ought not to be questioned. But if we suppose that as a matter of fact no one has ever experienced what is usually called power, we suppose what is certainly false. It is probably false on the supposition that men like Locke or Leibniz described their experience adequately and found "power"; and on the ground of my own autobiography, I can assert that it is absolutely false. In the third place, Hume is unquestionably correct when he concludes that from the experience of power we can never pass to knowledge concerning instances of power not experienced. In other words, the observation of power does not establish necessary connection, any more than the observation of constant conjunction. If reasoning concerning matter of fact implies that the opposite of any reasoned conclusion is inconceivable, it is obvious that no experience can be the ground of any reasoning which concerns non-experienced entities.

Having shown that reason cannot justify the belief that any particular cause must necessarily have a particular effect, Hume proposes to consider any other possible grounds for this belief. It is unnecessary for our purposes to review what he says about belief and its *causes*. He articulates the principles of the association of ideas and prepares to explain the origin of the belief in necessary connection.[1] He tells us that the belief that any particular cause must have a particular effect arises from habit or custom. The experience of a series of conjoined objects creates upon the subsequent appearance of one of these objects the belief in the existence of the other. From this conclusion, the answer to the main question can easily be drawn. ". . . the manner in which we reason beyond our immediate impressions, and conclude that such particular causes must have such particular effects"[2] has been explained. The main question asks more generally: "What is our idea of necessity when we say that two objects are necessarily connected together?"[3] Hume's answer to this general question is identical with his answer to the particular question. "For, after a frequent repetition, I find that upon the appearance of one of the objects the mind is determined by custom to consider its usual attendant, and to consider it in a stronger light upon account of its relation to the first object. It is this impression, then, or determination, which affords me the idea of necessity."[4]

The concept of the "determination of the mind" involves Hume in a dilemma. The phrase undoubtedly refers to a causal action of past impressions. If this causal relation involves necessary connection, Hume is admitting cases of necessary connection between impressions or finite existents. Given a number of experiences of conjoined objects, is the subsequent

---

[1] It seems to me clearly the case that in his discussion of the "causes of belief" Hume is not considering cause in the sense of necessary connection, but in the sense of efficacy. He uses terms such as force and vivacity, production, efficacy, persuasion, etc., terms which all serve to convey the notion of active influence.

[2] *Treatise*, I, 153.   [3] Ibid.   [4] Ibid., 154.

inference from one to the other necessary? This cannot be the case. There is nothing inconceivable about the notion of having any number of such experiences and yet not drawing such an inference. Hume cannot mean by "determination of the mind" and by "give rise to a new idea" and by "produce a new impression" that impressions and ideas are necessarily connected, if his discussion of necessary connection is to be taken seriously. To avoid this conclusion Hume must choose the other horn of the dilemma. He must regard the phrase "determination of the mind" as referring not to a necessary connection of impressions but to a *causal or productive* relation between impressions. I take it, therefore, that he substituted the notion of causation as production for the idea of necessary connection in discussing the relations of impressions and belief. Our belief in the necessity of causes is explained by introducing a notion of causation other than that of necessity. If Hume shifts his meaning unconsciously and no explicit recognition of the shift is indicated, that is because Hume was interested in questions of necessary connection, not in questions of causal action. The dilemma can be briefly and exactly stated: Either Hume is asserting a necessary connection between impressions and belief, or he is asserting the existence of a causal relation unrelated to the idea of necessary connection. The second horn Hume must reject because he defined the causal relation as involving necessary connection and not because of any difficulty inherent in the assertion itself. But the first horn is meaningless in any context or regardless of context. It is obvious that the necessity of a belief is a special case of necessary connection. If the belief is distinct from the past experiences upon which it is based, it cannot be held to be necessary. Hence, if Hume means anything by "determination of the mind," he must be referring to a relationship which has nothing to do with necessary connection. If Hume wishes to restrict the term "causation" to cases of necessary connection, impressions cannot be considered to be causally related to beliefs. Yet Hume writes a chapter on "the *causes* of belief." He is here not using the term "cause" in the sense of necessary connection but in the sense of efficacy and power. "I would willingly establish it as a general maxim in the science of human nature, *that when any impression becomes present to us, it not only transports the mind to such ideas as are related to it, but likewise communicates to them a share of its force and vivacity.*"[1] As a description of the causal relations of impressions, this maxim of Hume's seems to me to be sound. Impressions are causally related to beliefs in the sense that the force and vivacity of certain ideas or impressions are transmitted to other ideas or impressions. This is a description of the causal relation; but it does not follow that we have here an instance of necessary connection. Hume seems here definitely to have chosen the second horn of the dilemma.

In terms of Hume's own analysis, necessary connection is dismissed and causal efficacy is retained. From any actual experienced causal connection between impressions we can draw no inferences regarding either the necessity of any belief or the belief in necessary connection. Our idea of necessity is nothing more

[1] *Treatise*, I, 101. Italics Hume's.

than an expectation which is causally related to past impressions, i.e. we have no idea of necessity at all. But this is not Hume's conclusion. He supposes that his discussion has in some sense justified the belief in scientific determinism. Hence, he concludes his discussion by laying down the rules of causal inference: "The same cause always produces the same effect, and the same effect never arises but from the same cause.... For as like causes always produce like effects, when in any instance we find our expectation to be disappointed, we must conclude that this irregularity proceeds from some difference in the causes."[1]

To assert that the "same cause always produces the same effect" is to assert necessary connection.[2] If the same cause always produces the same effect, then given the cause we can, before the occurrence of the effect, have certain knowledge of the effect. There are three different senses, however, in which this rule may be interpreted. If it is regarded as a proposition about the world it may or may not be true. The discovery of even one instance in which the same cause is not followed by the same effect would make it false. Hume does not think that this is the case. Whatever experience discloses, any apparent "irregularity proceeds from some difference in the cause." In other words, Hume does not think that the proposition "same cause, same effect" could be shown to be false, and thus we must conclude that it is not a genuine proposition. Secondly, it may be regarded as expressing a prejudice of Hume's. If it were such an expression it could not be significantly argued. Thirdly, it may

[1] *Treatise*, I, 170–1.
[2] "... like effects *necessarily* follow from like causes." Ibid., 171.

be offered as a necessary truth concerning nature. In this case a ground is supplied upon which apparent irregularities can be dismissed from consideration. It is undoubtedly the case that Hume held this third view. If, however, this rule is to be considered as a necessary truth, it must be so because of intuition or demonstration. According to Hume the only relations which give rise to intuitive certainty are comparisons of ideas. "These relations are resemblance, proportions in quantity and number, degrees of quality and contrariety; none of which are implied in this proposition...."[1] that the same cause will always have the same effect. But if this proposition cannot be called intuitively certain, neither can it be demonstrated. The opposite of any demonstrated conclusion is inconceivable. There is nothing inconceivable about different effects following from the same causes, or about the same effects following from different causes.[2] Hume can only reply here by falling back upon the second interpretation, namely, that regardless of the lack of evidence, intuition or demonstration, he chooses to assert this rule. Hence nothing more need be said. I believe that I have finally shown that Hume's "scepticism" never extended so far as his own naïve faith in the truth of determinism.

If the causal action of past impressions does not involve necessity, then the absence of the belief in necessary connection from the mind of any individual (e.g. anyone who believes in chance or freedom) is conceivable. But Hume's attack on those who denied

---

[1] *Treatise*, I, 82.
[2] In a later chapter I shall return to a consideration of this maxim, "same cause, same effect."

necessity and asserted freedom seems to be evidence that he regarded the belief in necessity as a necessary consequence of certain sequences of experience. In other words, Hume seems to be saying that the belief in necessary connection is itself necessary. The difficulty in attempting to understand how any belief can be necessary results from a type of confusion which is common in Hume. Critics of Hume[1] have pointed out that Hume confused a "repetition of impressions" with an "impression of repetition," an "idea of infinity" with an "infinite idea," and an "idea of length" with the "length of an idea." In his discussion of necessity there is a similar confusion. He confuses a "belief in necessary connection" with a "necessary belief in connection." In terms of his own argument, a belief in necessary connection or determinism is nonsense; but determinism is saved by discovering that the belief in the regular sequence of events is itself necessary.

The analysis of the "belief in necessary connection" discloses either (1) that the belief is meaningless because its object is meaningless, or (2) that such a belief is self-contradictory. If no meaning can be given to the idea of necessary connection, then no meaning can be given to the *belief* in such a connection. If one attempts, however, to give a meaning to "necessary connection" in terms of certain knowledge, he converts the "belief in necessary connection" into a self-contradiction. If we know that two objects are necessarily connected then the knowledge of one is ground for certain knowledge as to the existence of the other. "Such an inference would amount to knowledge, and

[1] J. Laird, *Hume's Philosophy of Human Nature*, 129.

would imply the absolute contradiction and impossibility of conceiving anything different."[1] If two objects are not necessarily connected the inference from one to the other cannot be an affair of knowledge. In these terms, the belief in necessary connection means that we believe that the opposite of what we believe is contradictory and inconceivable. But in this case, such a belief would be knowledge. The point of the distinction between belief and knowledge is that the first provides for the possibility of error. This means that either we know that two objects are necessarily connected or we do not; the belief in their necessary connection is self-contradictory. Ultimately, it asserts, "I believe (and may be wrong in this belief) that there is no possibility of my being wrong."

It follows further, that the belief in the truth of determinism is also contradictory. The assertion of determinism implies the assertion of absolute knowledge. If we know that A determines B, we know that given the existence of A, it is inconceivable that B shall not exist; and we know this prior to the existence of B. The proposition "A causes B" describes an actual relationship between A and B; but the proposition "A determines B" says only that given A, B must also be given necessarily. It is possible significantly to *believe* that "A causes B"; for such a belief is only the belief in the existence of an actual state of affairs and in any given instance it may be false. But we cannot significantly *believe* that A determines B; for the proposition "A determines B" implies certain knowledge as to the relation of A and B. To believe that "A determines B," is to believe that we have certain knowledge

[1] *Treatise*, I, 89.

about the relation of A and B. But since a belief in certain knowledge is either nonsensical or contradictory, the belief in determinism is either nonsensical or contradictory.[1]

Since, as I have pointed out above, the necessity of a belief is but a special case of necessary connection, determinism cannot be saved by appealing to the necessity of a belief in determinism. Kant, however, attempts to do just this; he attempts to establish the necessity of certain beliefs by calling them categories of the human mind. All things must be conceived as determined because the category of determinism is a presupposition of knowledge. It will be noticed that I substitute the term determinism for Kant's term "causality." This substitution is justified since by causality Kant did not intend to denote any observable relation of phenomena, but the disposition of the mind to regard the succession of phenomena as necessary. As a category, the disposition of the mind to regard things as necessarily connected is itself a necessary presupposition of knowledge. Thus Kant combines into one doctrine the two doctrines which Hume confused. He asserts a necessary disposition (belief) to regard phenomena as necessarily connected.

[1] I shall return to this question in a later chapter, when I consider the materialists' belief in determinism or the "reign of law."

CHAPTER V

THE PERCEPTION OF CAUSAL EFFICACY

PASSAGES from Locke and Leibniz testifying to the perception of causal efficacy have already been quoted. I should like now to add the testimony of my own experience, which is, I am convinced, typical. My grounds for this conviction will be made clear below.

In examining my experiences I discover cases of causal efficacy: for example, I may be angry at one moment and calmer at the next. I not only perceive that the moment of calm follows the moment of anger, but I perceive the moment of calm rise out of the moment of anger. In the very moment of calm I perceive the influences of the previous feeling. The experience not only follows but inherits the emotional tones of past experience. In general, I perceive genuine causal influence when I become conscious of the relations of emotions and feelings. Regarding each feeling or emotion as an event, there is here an indubitable experience of the causal relation of events.

In many cases the causal influence may not be directly perceived. Under great emotional stress we are not inclined to introspect and observe the development of our emotions. Later we may attempt to remember and to reconstruct imaginatively the course of the development. Again, emotional influences may operate below the level of consciousness, and so be imperceptible. Finally, other interests may lead to a sublimation of emotions and feelings as, for example, when the experience is assumed to have future practical significance. Thus, in visual perception we are rarely concerned with the act of perception; our interest, instead, lies in the object perceived. This object informs us of surrounding objects and enables us to adjust our movements. It is only in cases of error in our practical life that our attention is turned from the object perceived to the act of perception. Though the causal relation is not always observed, we cannot assume that when it is not observed it ceases to exist. The only requirements for ostensive definition are that the entity denoted shall be observable, and observed at least once. Subsequently, we need not be confronted with instances of causation directly and consciously in order to make significant propositions about it. In other words, as I shall argue in more detail later, feeling and experience do not necessarily involve consciousness. Hence there can be no logical objection to the transition of emotional tones or influences below the level of consciousness.

The preceding two paragraphs contain what I take to be the gist of Whitehead's discussion of the perception of causal efficacy. Whitehead cites the immediate perception of the transition of emotion as evidence against Hume's conclusion that succession is the only perceived relation of impressions. "Hume appeals to a doctrine of force and liveliness as an essential factor in an impression of sensation. This doctrine is nothing but a special cause of the doctrine of subjective forms.[1] Again, he holds that the force and liveliness of one occasion of experience enter into the character of succeeding occasions. The whole doctrine of 'custom' depends on this assumption. If the occasions be entirely

[1] By "subjective forms" Whitehead means "emotional tone."

separate, as Hume contends, this transition of character is without any basis in the nature of things. What Hume, in his appeal to memory, is really doing is to appeal to an observed immanence of the past in the future, involving a continuity of subjective form. . . . But the conclusion follows that there is an observed relation of causation between such occasions. . . . The additional conclusion can also be derived, that in so far as we apply notions of causation to the understanding of events in nature, we must conceive these events under the general notions which apply to occasions of experience. For we can only understand causation in terms of our observation of these occasions. This appeal to Hume has the sole purpose of illustrating the common-sense obviousness of the present thesis."[1]

I think it fairly certain that Hume, had he not been concerned with questions of necessary connection but with the nature of causation, would also have testified to the "common-sense obviousness of this thesis." He says, "I would willingly establish it as a general maxim in the science of human nature, *that when any impression becomes present to us, it not only transports the mind to such ideas as are related to it, but likewise communicates to them a share of its force and vivacity.*"[2] Hume's difficulty lay in confusing "separation" in the sense of logical separation with separation in the sense of lack of causal connection. But if it is recognized that the assertion of causal connection is in no sense an assertion of necessary connection, Hume himself must be understood as testifying to the direct perception of causal efficacy.

[1] A. N. Whitehead, *Adventures of Ideas*, 236–7.
[2] *Treatise*, I, 101. Italics Hume's.

Another passage from Hume contains a seemingly innocent though very significant qualification of his method of investigating the nature of the causal relation. "I shall only observe before I proceed any further, that though the ideas of cause and effect can be derived from the impressions of reflection as well as from those of sensation, yet for brevity's sake I commonly mention only the latter as the origin of these ideas; though I desire that, whatever I say of them, may also extend to the former. Passions are connected with their objects and with one another; no less than external bodies are connected together. The same relation then of cause and effect, which belongs to one, must be common to all."[1] As a statement of method, this passage contains no argument against the procedure adopted by Whitehead, who, as we have seen, derives the notion of causation from non-sensuous impressions ("impressions of reflection") and argues that "in so far as we apply notions of causation to the understanding of events in nature, we must conceive these events under the general notions which apply to occasions of experience." Hume, on the other hand, begins with the observation of "external bodies" and generalizes the observed relations so that the passions can be understood to have similar relations. ("The same relation then, of cause and effect, which belongs to one, must be common to all.") Let us suppose, now, that in the observation of "external bodies" we only perceive succession, but that in the observation of the relation of the passions we perceive causal efficacy. The statement that the "relation . . . must be common" can then be interpreted as meaning

[1] *Treatise*, I, 81.

either of two things: (1) it may be taken as denying the existence of a relation of causal efficacy between impressions of reflection (passions); or (2) it may be taken as asserting an unperceived causal relation between "external bodies." Hume's method permits only the first interpretation, since he proposes to start from the observation of the relation of external bodies and to generalize on the basis of this observation. But the denial of something actually perceived must ultimately be devoid of meaning. Further, in his actual concern with impressions of reflection, Hume continually refers to the perception of causal efficacy.[1]

I should agree with Hume's conclusion that the ideas of cause and effect are not derived from impressions of sensation. The analysis of sense data will never disclose the perception of causal efficacy. It may have been for this reason that the philosophers of the seventeenth century followed what is the essence of Whitehead's procedure and derived the idea of causation from an internal impression. Such an internal impression can be made the ground for an inference regarding instances of causal efficacy not directly perceived. Thus Locke holds that "*The clearest idea of active power (is) had from spirit. We* are abundantly furnished with the idea of passive power by almost all sorts of sensible things. . . . Nor have we of active power (which is the more proper signification of the word 'power') fewer instances; since whatever change is observed, the mind must collect a power somewhere

[1] The second interpretation, the assertion of the existence of something unperceived, is not devoid of significance, providing that what is asserted to exist has been perceived in other circumstances. The assertion of the existence of an unperceived causal relation is always significant, though in any given case it may be false.

to make that change. . . . But yet if we will consider it attentively, bodies, by our senses, do not afford us so clear and distinct an idea of active power as we have from reflection on the operations of our own minds. . . . So that it seems to me we have, from the observation of bodies by our senses, but a very imperfect idea of active power, since they afford us *not any idea in themselves of the power to begin any action, either motion or thought.*"[1] When Locke says that in the case of the observation of the changes in moving bodies "the mind must collect a power" he means that no power is perceived and that the mind infers its presence. But we could not infer the presence of an unknown X; some experience must yield a direct experience of power if our inference to the existence of a non-observed power is to be meaningful.

I will attempt to show now that the philosophers of the seventeenth century who did not remain content with assertions of determinism and attempted to give an account of the causal relation, gave accounts essentially the same as the one I have given on the first page of this chapter or the one given by Whitehead. Hume's mistaken identification of causation and necessary connection has blinded subsequent investigators to the actual descriptions of the causal relation attempted by the thinkers of the seventeenth century.

---

[1] *Essay*, I, 164–5, italics mine. In another passage Locke states that from the observation of bodies it is also impossible to derive any idea of the manner in which motion is communicated from one body to another. "The coherence and continuity of the parts of matter; the production of sensation in us of colours and sounds, etc., by impulse and motion; *nay, the original rules and communication of motion being such, wherein we can discover no natural connexion with any ideas we have,* we cannot but ascribe them to the arbitrary will and good pleasure of the Wise Architect." *Essay*, IV, 455–6.

Windelband comments at length upon the almost universal dismissal of "final cause" from the explanations of nature which are found in the writings of seventeenth-century philosophers.[1] Spinoza's polemic against final causes[2] is perhaps the best known among these writings, but similar polemics are to be found in the writings of Descartes,[3] Bacon,[4] Hobbes,[5] etc. There was also, and this is usually overlooked, a marked tendency to dismiss the traditional efficient causes along with the final causes. Efficient causes were stigmatized under the name of "occult qualities." But no satisfactory notion of efficient causation could be found to replace the "occult qualities" and "substantial forms." It was thought that the discussion of efficient causes had no actual contribution to make to natural science. What was required for science was, instead, strict determinism and movement according to law; and this could most easily be secured by regarding God as the sole efficient cause.

However, when various thinkers did turn to the consideration of efficient causes, in one form or another the despised "occult causes" were reintroduced. Thus Galileo accuses Kepler of employing "occult causes" to explain the action of the moon upon the tides;[6] the Cartesians[7] and Leibniz[8] accuse the Newtonians of employing occult causes to explain natural phenomena; and Leibniz himself finds it necessary to reintroduce

---

[1] W. Windelband, *History of Philosophy*, 401 et seq.
[2] B. Spinoza, *Ethics*, I, Appendix.   [3] R. Descartes, *Works*, I, 173.
[4] F. Bacon, *De Augmentis*, III, 4.   [5] Hobbes, *Works*, I, 132.
[6] G. Galileo, *Two Great Systems*, 422.
[7] Cote's preface to the second edition of Newton's *Mathematical Princ.*, xxvi–xxvii.
[8] G. W. von Leibniz, *Correspondence with Clarke*, 187–9.

substantial forms in his descriptions of the activity of the monads. Even so dogmatic a materialist as Hobbes introduces the concept of "endeavour" to account for the action of one body on another.

The point of the attack on "occult causes" was that such causes were not perceived; rather they were postulated *ad hoc*. Hence the all-pervading ether with which the Cartesians sought to replace the Newtonian concept of gravitation must itself be regarded as an "occult cause." The Cartesians might answer that although they could not perceive the action of the ether, they could perceive the action of one body upon another, and hence the inference of the ether's existence is analogically justified, i.e. bodies are required to push stars, as on the terrestrial plane bodies are required to push other bodies. But by the same argument we perceive "occult qualities" or activities; as Gassendi[1] pointed out, in the case of the boy who was "attracted" by the apple, the experience of attraction and repulsion and their influence on subsequent actions is indubitable. May we then conclude that in cases where the "occult qualities" or attractions are not perceived they are nevertheless acting and are the causes of the phenomena? Of course, if matter is defined as that which possesses no occult qualities or efficacy, the attempt to account for the behaviour of matter in terms of occult qualities is no doubt contradictory. But this procedure makes the denial of the existence of "occult qualities" a matter of definition. Definitions, however, tell us nothing about existence; from the definition of the term matter we cannot conclude that anything resembling what is defined actually exists. Hence the

[1] Lange, *History of Materialism*, 266.

definition of matter cannot be an intelligible ground upon which to deny the existence of "occult qualities." But even if we admit the existence of "inactive masses," as Leibniz called the atoms,[1] what follows? With the elimination of "occult causes" we have eliminated efficient causes altogether. If matter is defined as dead or inert, not only is it impossible to understand how motion originates, but it is impossible to understand how motion is communicated in terms of matter alone. God is required to perform both functions.

Of all the thinkers of the seventeenth century, Leibniz, who most clearly recognized the limits and "easy beauty" of materialistic explanations, gave the most careful description of causal efficacy. "The activity of the internal principle which produces change or passage from one perception to another may be called Appetition. . . . Further, nothing but this, namely, perceptions and their changes can be found in a simple substance. It is also in this alone that all the internal activities of simple substances can consist."[2] Leibniz, in the interests of his pre-established harmony, restricts this activity to an internal process; but excepting this complication we have here a clear statement that causation designates a relation of efficacy (or efficacious influence) between perceptions or occasions of experience. Leibniz recognizes that we may not always be conscious of the causal relations of perceptions. I have said that the transference of emotions may sometimes take place below the level of consciousness; and Leibniz provides for this subliminal transference with

[1] "I have no knowledge of these idle, useless, and inactive masses . . ." *The Monadology and Other Philosophical Writings*, 326.
[2] Ibid., 226, 228–9.

his doctrine of "petites perceptions": "These petites perceptions have thus an influence greater than people think. It is they that form this something I know not what, these tastes . . . these connections which each being has with all the rest of the universe. It may even be said that in consequence of these petites perceptions the present is big with the future and laden with the past."[1] Leibniz's description of the causal relation seems clearly in agreement with the description given in the first paragraphs of this chapter. The events which constitute the life history of any individual exhibit not sheer succession but causal influence. This causal influence provides for the transmission of subjective form, and consequently "the present is big with the future and laden with the past."

The events whose connections Leibniz directly experiences are those events which constitute his own life history. It is from the observation of these events that Leibniz derives his notion of causation and activity. However, Leibniz on the basis of this direct experience concludes that the observed relations of perceptions or occasions of experience constitute the type of the causal relation: "It is also in this alone that all the internal activities of simple substances can consist." Since ultimately simple substances are the only existents, we may infer that there is no other kind of activity. Leibniz regarded mistaken notions concerning space and extension as the only reasons for denying the activity of substances. I mention this point in passing. I shall later examine Leibniz's dis-

[1] *The Monadology and Other Philosophical Writings*, introduction to "New Essays on the Human Understanding," 372–3.

cussion of extension in the consideration of the relation of succession. I may say here only that Leibniz regarded all substances as sentient, and space as a mode of togetherness of such substances. If all substances are sentient, we have no difficulty in conceiving causal action in general as a transition of emotion or activity. On this point Locke was opposed to Leibniz and accepted the two-substance cosmology of Descartes. Nevertheless, for Locke just as for Leibniz our idea of causation is not derivable from the consideration of bodies and is derivable from a consideration of sentient substances or spirits.

It is unfortunate that Leibniz's religious interests influenced and obscured his account of causation. He saw in the fact of appetition a ground for the doctrine of final causes. An appetite is usually an appetite for something, and this something can be regarded as the final cause of the appetite. "Souls act according to the laws of final causes through appetitions, means, and ends. Bodies act according to the laws of efficient causes and motions. And the two realms, that of efficient cause and that of final causes, are in harmony with one another."[1] This passage appears in an argument for the pre-established harmony, and it is plain that his interest in this thesis has caused Leibniz to forget his account of efficient causation. The statement that the two realms are in harmony with one another is evidence that Leibniz is here not concerned with the nature of the causal relation but with the order of nature. In the first place, regardless of the objects of the soul's appetites, the relation of these appetites to one another is that of efficient causation.

[1] *The Monadology and Other Philosophical Writings*, 263.

The internal activity of the monad is expressed in the causal (efficient) relations of its perceptions. Secondly, it is meaningless to say that "bodies act according to the laws of efficient causes" because bodies do not act. Ultimately there are no bodies, and the sole real activity consists in the relation of perceptions. Bodies may be understood as collections of simple substances, but there is no causal action, for Leibniz, between substances. The laws of motion are not statements of the operation of efficient causes but statements of the pre-established harmony.

A clear distinction between the laws of motion and the notion of efficient causation is to be found in the writings of Newton. We have seen that he did not consider the *Principia* to be concerned with physical causes, though it is undoubtedly concerned with the laws of motion. When Newton comes to examine the actual nature of efficient causes, like Leibniz and Locke, he employs the notion of spirit. "And now we might add something concerning a certain most subtle spirit which pervades and lies hid in all gross bodies by the force and action of which spirit the particles of bodies attract one another at near distances, and cohere, if contiguous; and electric bodies operate to greater distances, as well repelling as attracting neighbouring corpuscles; and light is emitted, reflected, refracted, inflected, and heats bodies; and all sensation is excited . . . etc."[1] Newton does not refer to these subtle spirits in explaining the grand movements of the heavenly bodies. For the order of these movements God is the efficient cause. But God differs from these "most subtle spirits" only in His infinity and immensity.

[1] *Principia*, III, General Scholium, 547.

In either case it is a spirit that is the efficient cause. Newton does not employ the notion of spirits to account for the transmission of motion by impact; but if these spirits lie hid in *all* gross bodies, one may infer that the transmission of motion is due to the activity of these spirits. As we have said, Newton does not add any further statements to the suggestion quoted above; but this passage seems in itself sufficient evidence that Newton thought that force and action involved the concept of spirit. At least, this must stand as Newton's only attempt to give a physical account of causation. I use the term physical here not as synonymous with material but as opposed to mathematical.

Neither Locke nor Newton seem willing to follow out their concept of activity to the point where the existence of "gross material bodies" is denied. But both are certain that the idea of active power is derived from a consideration of spirit. "Whether matter be wholly destitute of active power as its author God is truly above all passive power; and whether the intermediate states of created spirits be not alone capable of both active and passive power is worth consideration. I shall not now enter into that inquiry. . . . But since active powers make so great a part of our complex ideas of natural substances (as we shall see hereafter), and I mention them as such according to common apprehension; yet they being not, perhaps, so truly active powers as our hasty thoughts are apt to represent them, I judge it not amiss, by this intimation, to direct our minds to the consideration of God and spirits for the clearest idea of active power."[1] This passage

[1] *Essay*, 164.

illustrates how close Locke was to Leibniz on important points of doctrine. Locke says that a large part of our ideas of natural substances is made up of the idea of active power. But since he believed in the existence of substance defined in terms of extension (and solidity), he is forced to say that the attribution of active power to all natural substances is mistaken. Had he possessed Leibniz's insight into the nature of extension and spatial relations, he would have retained the initial insight that active power makes up a large part of our idea of natural substances, and would have given up his belief in dead material substance.

Even Malebranche testifies directly and indirectly to the observed activity of spirits. He accepts not only the Cartesian definition of matter but also the assertion of the existence of matter so defined, and concludes that we can have no idea of the existence of power or efficacy so long as we confine our attention to matter. But Malebranche also accepted the Cartesian concept of spirit as a result of which he is led to ascribe power to spirits: "To understand this rightly, we must know, there's a very considerable difference between the impression of motion the Author of nature produces in matter and the impression of motion towards good in general wherewith the same Author of nature continually influences our soul: For matter is wholly inactive; it has no power of retarding, or stopping its motion, or determining and turning it one way rather than another. . . . But 'tis not so with the will, which may in one sense be said to be active, and to have a *power* in itself of giving a different determination to the inclination or impression it receives from God."[1]

[1] *Search After Truth*, 3.

The doctrine expressed here is no doubt inconsistent with Malebranche's occasionalistic and deterministic conclusions, but Malebranche seems aware of this inconsistency, and it is responsible for the *non sequitur* by which he tries to prove that God is the sole cause. "It is evident that all bodies, great and little, have not force to move themselves. . . . Since therefore our idea of bodies convinces us that they cannot move themselves, we must conclude that they are moved by spirits. But considering our idea of finite spirits, we see no necessary connection betwixt their will and the motion of any body whatsoever . . ."[1] From this argument Malebranche concludes that no finite things possess power of any sort. It is obvious that there is no parallel between Malebranche's discussion of matter and his discussion of spirit. A genuine argument denying activity or power to both matter and spirit should have proceeded, in brief, in this order: "It is evident that all bodies great and little have not force to move themselves, and it is also evident that all spirits have no force to move themselves." If Malebranche had used this argument, his conclusion that God is the sole active cause would follow. But the fact that Malebranche explicitly ascribes power to spirits (in the first passage quoted above) and finds it necessary to shift his ground (in the second) and begin to talk about necessary connection rather than power, seems to indicate that he felt it impossible to deny power to spirits.

If we compare what Spinoza says about the relations of bodies with what he says about the activity of minds, we can see that he too derived his notions of efficacy

[1] *Search After Truth*, 55.

from the latter. It is true that Spinoza is not particularly concerned with the concept of causation; but in so far as he is the concept receives content from a consideration not of bodies but of the actions and passions of man. In his discussion of the movements of bodies he asserts only that their movements are determined, and not that one body is the cause of the movement of the other. This is not always apparent from the propositions, but it is apparent from the manner in which the propositions are demonstrated. "Lemma III. A body in motion or at rest must be determined to motion or rest by another body, which was also determined to motion or rest by another, and that in its turn by another, and so on, *ad infinitum*."[1] Superficially, this seems to be a statement that one body is the cause of the movement of the other; yet this is not, I think, what is intended by Spinoza. If bodies are regarded as causes, the order of bodily movements should be derivable from a consideration of bodies alone. Spinoza's demonstration of this Lemma, however, says nothing about one body being a cause of the movement of another; what he does say is that bodies, being individual modes of God's attribute of extension, are determined as described in proposition 28, part I. But in the proof of proposition 28, part I, Spinoza derives the determinate series of finite things from the immanent causality of God, and not from the causal activity of the finite things. That is to say, there is nothing in the nature of finite bodies alone from which it follows that one shall be determined (or caused) to movement or rest by another.

In the corollary to Lemma III, Spinoza states the

[1] *Ethics*, Pt. II, 62.

THE PERCEPTION OF CAUSAL EFFICACY 171

first law of motion and asserts its self-evidence. "Hence it follows that a body in motion will continue in motion until it be determined to a state of rest by another body, and that a body at rest will continue at rest until it be determined to a state of motion by another body. This indeed is self-evident."[1] In this assertion of self-evidence we may suppose that Spinoza has left the protection of any reference to God's omnipotence, and we can examine this statement on its merits. What are its merits? In the first place it is possible to maintain the self-evidence of this law by regarding it as a definition. Thus if we perceive that any entity changes from rest to motion or from motion to rest without observing any cause of this change, Spinoza can assert that such entities are not what he means by bodies. He will regard as bodies only those entities whose behaviour falls within the limits of his definition. Secondly, it is not a satisfactory definition, since one of its most important terms has no meaning, that is, the term "determined." What is meant by the statement that one body determines another to either motion or rest? Spinoza can give no meaning to this term other than that got by referring to the proposition which tells us that the regular movement of bodies follows from God's determining them to act in a certain manner. But we are supposing here that the first law of motion is self-evident without reference to God. Hence without reference to God all that Spinoza can say is that the movement of one body follows the movement of any body it does happen to follow.[2]

[1] *Ethics*, Pt. II, 62.
[2] Eddington restates the first law of motion to assert: "Every body continues in its state of rest or uniform motion in a straight line, except in so far as it doesn't."

Thirdly, if we regard the law as a generalization of descriptions of empirical fact and disregard its claims to self-evidence, it seems obviously false. Two instances which illustrate its falsity can be given here: when we direct or change the motion of our bodies we make false that part of the law which asserts that only a body can determine the movement of another body; when we observe the acceleration of a freely falling body that part of the law which asserts uniform motion is also shown to be false.[1]

We may conclude, then, that no account of the causal relation is contained in Spinoza's discussion of body. But when he comes to consider the nature of the mind and will he asserts a perception of efficacy or activity. "The mind, both in so far as it has clear and distinct ideas, and in so far as it has confused ideas, endeavours to persevere in its being for an indefinite time, and *is conscious of this effort*."[2] He continues in the scholium of this proposition to describe the nature of this "effort." "This effort, when it is related to the mind alone, is called will, but when it is related at the same time both to the mind and body is called 'appetite,' which is therefore nothing but the very essence of man . . ."[3] It should be noticed that Leibniz merely generalizes this notion and holds that appetite is the essence of finite substances in general. It may be objected here that the things which Spinoza says about man are inconsistent with his views concerning God or his "metaphysics." I can only answer that it remains the case that when Spinoza

---

[1] I shall return to the discussion of the "first law of motion" in the following chapter.
[2] *Ethics*, Pt. III, prop. ix, 115. [3] Ibid.

comes to talk of man he introduces terms like "conatus," "effort," "activity" and "passion," and asserts that man is active in so far as he is the cause of changes in his environment and passive in so far as he is affected by his environment. Spinoza does not merely attest to the existence of a causal relation; he gives the relation content in terms of the appetites, actions, and passions of men. And these appetites, actions, and passions are matters of which we are conscious (at least sometimes), and hence we have direct knowledge of the nature of the causal relation. It is, thus, the consciousness of our own activities and passions which gives empirical content to the causal relation.

Hobbes, unlike the majority of his contemporaries, held that the movement of one body could be the efficient cause of the movement of another. But even he introduces such terms as "endeavour" and "to press" and "resistance"; terms which can be given meaning only so far as they refer to a sentient substance. He attempts to define endeavour so that it can be understood in terms of bodies alone; but the notion of causal efficacy is introduced by the imagery which is usually excited by the term, and which Hobbes' redefinition fails to dissolve. His definition is the following: "First, I define endeavour to be motion made in less space and time than can be given; that is, less than can be determined or assigned by exposition or number; that is, motion made through the length of a point, and in an instant, or point of time . . ."[1] It is to be noticed that no implication of power or causal efficacy is to be found in the definition.[2]

[1] *Works*, I, 206.

[2] The notion of infinitesimals is suggested and in a manner crude enough to exhibit the difficulties which the calculus is successful in hiding.

However, Hobbes uses the notion of endeavour to account for the "action" of one body on another: "Fourthly, that I may define what it is to press, I say that of two moved bodies one presses the other, when with its endeavour it makes either all or part of the other body to go out of its place."[1] But what is there about endeavour as defined which involves pressures or could *make* another body move? Clearly, there is no notion of efficiency involved in motion through a point and for an instant. In what sense can such a motion *make* another body do anything? To say that it "presses" the other body says nothing, since we must ask what is meant by one body pressing another. We can, I suppose, define "endeavour," "press," and "make" in terms of one another; but unless one or the other is defined ostensively the terms cease to have empirical or existential significance. Hobbes' argument gains plausibility only because his readers tend to supply content to these terms by referring them to their own experiences of effort, resistance, and pressure. These terms have concrete meaning only as applied to descriptions of sentient substance. Hence, if by "body" Hobbes means sentient substance, his analysis has meaning. But if, what is more likely, he meant by "body" the traditional dead material substance, he fails to give an account which is empirically significant of the causal relation of bodies.

I shall conclude this discussion of seventeenth-century thinkers with an examination of Descartes' implicit theory of efficient causation. Usually he is content to regard God as the sole efficient cause; but it should be noticed that while he finds no difficulty

[1] *Works*, I, 211.

in reconciling the behaviour of matter with the notion that God is the sole cause, he does find difficulty in reconciling God as the sole cause with the activity of spirits. The essence of matter is exhausted in extension; from the consideration of matter we can derive no idea of causation or efficacy. On the other hand, the freedom of spirits is a basic or self-evident truth for Descartes. It is for him a matter of direct experience that spirits exert causal influence, though Descartes substitutes the term "freedom" for causal influence.

If we suppose that for Descartes the concept of freedom involved the concept of power, then in admitting the direct evidence of freedom Descartes admits the direct evidence of power. It seems to me plain that the preceding inference is justified inasmuch as Descartes means by freedom that men can will to do thus and so. If, however, we suppose that the inference is not justified and that Descartes, unlike Locke, regarded the idea of power and freedom as distinct, it still remains true that Descartes never attempted to derive the idea of causal efficacy from the concept of extension or the observation of bodies. On this interpretation I should conclude that Descartes had no theory as to the nature of the causal relation.

Returning now to the passage from Hume quoted above (page 158), is it not apparent that Hume's procedure is designed not to find causal efficacy but to rule it out before the search begins? He says: "I shall observe before I proceed any further that the ideas of cause and effect can be derived from impressions of reflection *as well as from those of sensation*, yet for brevity's sake I commonly mention the latter as the origin of these ideas . . ."[1] Since by impressions of sensation Hume means the observation of "external bodies," it is obvious that in restricting his investigation to impressions of sensation Hume has already eliminated causal efficacy. It would be difficult to find a seventeenth-century philosopher (or a modern one) who would suppose that the ideas of cause and effect are derivable from impressions of sensation. As a statement of the origin of our ideas of cause and effect Leibniz, Newton, Spinoza, Malebranche, Descartes, and Locke would have regarded the above passage as false. Perhaps Hume only meant that he could so derive the idea of cause and effect. But if so, his failure to find causal efficacy means only that he cannot so derive it, and not that we have no idea of causal efficacy.

I wish to refer at this point to a modern philosopher who begins his analysis of causation by denying causal efficacy. C. D. Broad, in *Perception, Physics, and Reality*, argues in this way: "Can anything be made of this activity view? Let us take the law of causality first. All that is actually open to investigation in it can be stated in terms of the uniformity view. *For all that possibly could be observed on any theory is the changes in various things and their temporal relations to each other.*"[2] If this statement means that in observing change and succession we only observe change and succession, it is a tautology. If it means, however, that experience can be exhaustively described in terms of observed successions, uniform or otherwise, it is false. That is, it must be regarded as false unless one wishes to hold that Locke, Leibniz, Descartes, Spinoza, Whitehead, and others are deliberately attempting to deceive us

---

[1] *Treatise*, I, 81. [2] Op. cit., 79–80.

when they report the observation of activity. But several pages along in his argument Broad slightly modifies his statement, and apparently admits that there is a perception of activity. "Activity certainly cannot be observed in the external world. We can only observe those regularities from which we infer causal laws in the sense of the uniformity theory. . . . With regard to the so-called feeling of activity it seems almost certain that it depends upon the fact that we are minds and in volition produce states in our bodies which are causally connected with certain feelings in our minds. Hence if activity be identified with feeling of activity, there can be no reason to believe that it is a general characteristic of causation unless we are convinced on other grounds of an idealism like that of Leibniz, or Lotze or McTaggart, which holds that all substances are minds."[1] In the first place, Leibniz did not hold that all substances are minds, and it does not follow from the hypothesis that activity "is a general characteristic of all causation" that all substances are minds. It follows only that all substances must be capable of feeling. This is an important distinction; we may suppose that amoebae or electrons are capable of feeling without supposing that they are minds. In the second place, and this is the point of the quotation which makes it important for our discussion, Broad modifies his prior conclusion that only "the changes in various things and their temporal relations to each other" can be observed. In the second passage he holds that this limitation upon what we observe is true only so far as observations of the "external world" are concerned. The agreement of

[1] C. D. Broad, *Perception, Physics and Reality*, 89.

Broad with Hume on this point is apparent; Broad merely substitutes the phrase "external world" for "external bodies." The only legitimate conclusion for Broad or Hume is that there are two different kinds of substances or series of events; in one series we observe that the events merely succeed one another more or less uniformly, whereas in the other series there is a transition of activity.[1] This in effect is Locke's conclusion; we observe the operation of spiritual substance, but we do not observe the operation of material substance. However, Locke supposes that in the case of the relations of material substances the mind infers that God is the active cause.

Leibniz, however, believes that we have no grounds for the assertion of the existence of any substances incapable of feeling. Hence he concludes that activity is an ubiquitous character of the causal relation.[2]

Returning to the second quotation from Broad, what can be meant by the assertion that "activity certainly cannot be observed in the *external world*"? The difficulty lies in fixing the meaning of the phrase "external world." If Broad means by the external world the extended colour of a visual sense datum, his denial that we observe activity in the external world is non-significant. No one ever supposed that

---

[1] Hume, however, cannot accept the half-way house of dualism. He commits himself to the view that there can be no difference between the two series so far as the causal relations of the elements are concerned: "The same relation, then, of cause and effect which belongs to one, must be common to all."

[2] This, of course, is only true of the series of events that constitute the monad. Leibniz does deny that there is a transition of activity so far as the relations of monads are concerned. But this denial in no sense follows from the supposition of the existence of dead material substances. Rather, as we have seen, it is a consequence of his determinism.

THE PERCEPTION OF CAUSAL EFFICACY

activity is seen with the eyes or is an extended colour patch. If Broad means by "external world" the "real world," surely he cannot significantly deny that the causal relations of the events which constitute the life history of any sentient individual are parts of the real world. What Broad must mean is that only visual perception can be made the ground for an inference to the relation of events not directly perceived or existing independently of the act of perception. This is the only interpretation consistent with Broad's own doctrine of sensa and his acceptance of the causal theory of perception. Hence the fact that activity is not a visual sense datum would mean that we cannot use the perception of activity as the grounds for an inference concerning the relations of events not directly perceived or existing independently of the act of perception.

That we may see clearly what Broad intends, let us take two experiences or perceptions, A and B. A is to stand for the experience of succession, or what has traditionally been called "the billiard-ball situation"; B is to stand for the direct experience of the transmission of "force and liveliness" from one event to another. Which perception shall be made the basis of inferences concerning the nature of the causal relationships in the "external world"? Broad chooses the former. Let us analyse the "billiard-ball" situation to determine whether or not it can intelligently be made the ground for such an inference.

The proposition "x causes y" expresses a dyadic relationship; on the other hand, the proposition "x is followed by y" is really elliptical, since the relation of succession involves three terms. The unambiguous assertion of the succession of x and y is the proposition

"x is followed by y for z." The full description of the billiard-ball situation is not "x is followed by y," but "I observe that x is followed by y" or "Hume observes that x is followed by y" or "z observes that x is followed by y." The observation, whether mine, Hume's, or z's, is itself an event. Hence the relation of succession is triadic: "within event z, x is followed by y."

If this analysis holds, it follows that the relation of succession is only abstractly a relation between entities, and that concretely it is a relation within an event. As a concrete or existential fact, succession is always succession within an event. It is possible, however, for certain purposes to disregard the event within which the succession falls. This disregard for concrete fact is properly termed abstraction. Abstractions do not exist *qua* abstractions; hence to talk of succession as taking place or as existing outside of a percipient event (in the "external world") is entirely fallacious.[1] Before exhibiting the consequences of this conclusion for a doctrine of causation I wish to consider in some detail objections to this conclusion. In answering these objections I believe that the conclusion which I have stated so briefly will receive proper elucidation. The general objection can be stated: events or objects observed are external to the percipient event, and hence succession is not a relation within an event.

The objection cannot be maintained without main-

---

[1] "Abstract" is used here in the sense in which Leibniz uses it when he denies the existence of extended substance. Space, for Leibniz, is an abstraction, and since succession is a spatial relation (I am here referring to the billiard-ball situation) it too must be abstract. To say that space is abstract, and yet to insist that a spatial relation is concrete, is to say with Hobbes that space is a phantasm and yet that the contents of the phantasm are real.

taining a doctrine of absolute or, what is the same thing, of empty space and time. If succession is observed, the succession is quite literally within the percipient event. This last expresses an empirical fact. But many of our habits of speech have been developed under the aegis of absolutistic doctrines of space and time. For example, most of us would admit that time is abstracted from events. But if this is so, what meaning can be assigned to the proposition that "events are *in* time"? Derivatively events are in time, but the derivation expresses an abstraction from the event which contains the time. Apart from the event that endures, that is, that event in which the succession occurs, succession is meaningless. The proposition "events are in time," if taken as expressing or asserting a concrete fact about nature, is, to speak bluntly, nonsense. The conclusion that time is within events is directly in accord with much traditional philosophy; Bradley and Spinoza go only one step farther to the denial of the reality of events, and hence of the reality of time. However, in asserting that succession is always within an event, a reference is made to space as well as time. Here Bradley and Spinoza would differ. Bradley recognized that spatial relations must fall within some unity, a unity which I have referred to as the percipient event. Spinoza, on the contrary, held a theory of the existence or subsistence of absolute extension, i.e. he held that extension divorced from any particular event is an attribute of nature, and as such must be conceived through itself. Now, in asserting that what is perceived is spatially as well as temporally within an event, absolute extension is denied. If events or objects are observed, it is plainly the case that they are in perceptual space, and perceptual space is within the percipient event. However, a distinction may be made between physical and perceptual space, and it may be asserted that the event or objects observed are physically external to the percipient event. This brings us back to the ambiguity noticed in Broad's use of the term "external." If by definition physical space is other than perceptual space, then the experience of succession, since it involves nothing but perceptual space, tells us nothing about the nature of "external" or physical spatial relations. But further, I think the duplication of spaces, implied in the distinction between physical and perceptual space, is meaningless. I do not see how any proposition which asserts the existence of "physical space" can be given any significance. No more than in dealing with time can we say that "events are in space." What is the nature of the "space" in which we locate events? Try if you can to think of sheer extended nothingness between events. For myself, I do not require the aid of modern physics to convince me that such terms are intrinsically nonsense. But I am not denying the reality of extension or betweenness. Extension or space expresses the way in which objects are together in experience, i.e. within a percipient event. The proposition "events are in space" is a short-hand expression for the experience of togetherness. There is no togetherness, spatial or temporal, which is not the togetherness within a percipient event.

There is nothing novel about this doctrine. It was expressed by Leibniz repeatedly in controversies with the absolutists of his day. When he says that space is nothing but "the order of co-existence" he expresses the essence of the doctrine outlined above. Many thinkers might suppose that it is possible to accept Leibniz's doctrine (a relational view of space), and yet hold that nothing need be said about any percipient events. But such a view is plausible only because it leaves the nature of the entities which co-exist unspecified. Leibniz's whole point in reducing space to a relation of co-existence was to show that the substances or actually existing entities could not have as their essence space or extension. To say that space is the order of co-existing spaces is nonsense. Hence Leibniz found the essence of the entities which co-existed to be perception, or appetition.

I add several references to the conclusions of modern physical theory. I make no pretensions at understanding the experiments and mathematical manipulation which have led to the conclusions; but if the conclusions as stated agree with the deliverances of my own experience, I may quote them in support of my argument. The word "succession" is not used in these quotations; but the terms "length" and "duration" are, and if there is neither length nor duration "external" to the observer, then neither is succession external to the observer. If we observe that the movement of one billiard ball is followed in space and time by the movement of another, we certainly do observe just that. But Broad, and others, mean more by "external" than the extended quality of a visual field. They mean by "external world" the world existing independently of an act of perception. But if we eliminate the observer or the act of experience, we eliminate likewise the length, the duration, and the relation of succession.

Quoting Mr. Russell: "But relativity informs us that there is a residue of variability in measures which cannot be eliminated because, *in fact, the relations we try to measure are partially non-existent*. Or more correctly, they are relations involving more terms than we thought they did."[1] This passage summarizes my whole discussion of succession. By partially non-existent Mr. Russell means what I mean and what I take Leibniz to mean by "abstract." Considered by itself the relation of succession does not exist. More correctly, what exists involves more terms than is usually supposed, that is to say, what exists is "the perception of the succession."

Quoting Eddington: "Thus length and duration are not things inherent in the external world; they are relations of things in the external world to some specified observer. If we grasp all this, the mystery disappears from the phenomena described in Chapter 1. When the rod in the Michelson-Morley experiment is turned through a right angle it contracts; that naturally gives the impression that something happens to the rod itself. Nothing whatever has happened to the rod—the object in the external world. Its length has altered, but length is not an intrinsic property of the rod, since it is quite indeterminate until some observer is specified. We have been leading up from the older physics to the new outlook of relativity, and the reader may feel some doubt as to whether the strange phenomena of contraction and time retardation that were described in the last chapter are to be taken seriously, or are part of a *reductio ad absurdum* argument. The answer is that we believe the

[1] B. Russell, *Analysis of Matter*, 337. Italics mine.

phenomena do occur as described; only the description (like that of all observed phenomena) concerns the relation of the external world to some observer and not the external world itself. The startling character of the phenomena arises from the natural but fallacious inference that they involve intrinsic changes in the objects themselves."[1]

Turning now to situation B, namely the perception of causal efficacy, we find there a perceived transmission of "force and liveliness" or of emotional influence from one occasion of experience to another. Regarding these two occasions of experience as events in nature, there is a direct perception of the causal relation between such events. Here no third term is required, since one of the terms of the relation is a percipient event. To be sure in discussing this relation of causation we may find another event or several to be involved, but the point is that this other event is not essential to the existence of the relationship of the first two events. In the billiard-ball situation the observer is a constituent part of the event. In the causal situation the relation of the third event is not essential, since a percipient event is already provided as one of the terms in the causal relation. Thus the experience of the causal relation gives us direct knowledge of the relation of two events. We have seen that the experience of succession does not give us such knowledge. If we wish to know the nature of the relation between the unperceived entities which cause our perception of succession in the billiard-ball situation, we can argue analogically from our direct perception of causal efficacy and assert the existence of the same kind of relation.

[1] A. S. Eddington, *Space, Time and Gravitation*, 34.

Let us recapitulate. There are two experiences, one the experience of succession, another the experience of causal efficacy; we wish to know which experience can be made the grounds for the determination of the nature of the relation between unperceived entities or entities external to the act of perception. If we wish to know the nature of the relationship between two entities, one of which we say is the cause of the other, we cannot say they *succeed* one another for the following reasons: (1) Succession is a three-termed relation expressing the relation of two entities to a third, and not to each other; (2) the complex of characters which we designate as succession are not "intrinsic characters of the external world." On the other hand, we can say that what we mean by the assertion that one is the cause of the other is that their relationship is analogous to our own experience of causal efficacy; that is to say, that there is a transmission of energy, of "force and liveliness" from one entity to the other. The fact that we do not perceive this transmission of activity in the billiard-ball situation is here irrelevant. The question concerns the nature of the causal relation in the "external world," and not a description of visual perception. If the totality of "billiard-ball situations" exhausted the whole of experience—that is, if all our time was spent in observing moving colour patches—we would never know anything about the character of the external world. Thus Eddington says that the changes in visual phenomena ("the extended character of the rod") are not intrinsic changes of the objects in the external world.

The view I am upholding concerning the nature of the causal relation no doubt requires the assertion that all substances are capable of feeling. But once it is recognized that the character of visual perception cannot be made the ground of any conclusions concerning the nature of substances there is nothing which stands in the way of accepting such an assertion except traditional prejudice. I have attempted to show that perceptual extension does not involve the assertion of the existence of extended substance, but rather that extension is a relation within a percipient event. When Eddington says that extension is not an intrinsic character of the rod, he too is denying the existence of independently existing extended substances. Broad's statement that "activity certainly cannot be observed in the external world" tacitly presupposes that our observation of the external world consists in visual perception. The examination of this tacit presupposition discloses that the "succession" view of causation has little to recommend it. It does not follow that there is no observation or direct perception of the external world. In the experience of causal efficacy there is the direct perception of an event external to the act of perception, that is to say, there is a direct perception of the external world. The point to be grasped here is that "externality" cannot be understood in spatial terms, since the essence of extension or space does not lie in the fact that it divides entities but in the fact that it is the mode of togetherness of objects within an act of perception. The meaning of externality lies in the notion of existential independence. And the only kinds of entities whose existential independence of any act of perception can be significantly asserted are other acts of perception.

I add here a brief account of the genesis of the

notion that what exist external to any act of perception are material bodies or sheer extension. A fuller account of the doctrine of material substance will be given in the next chapter, but some consideration of the topic is required here in order to conclude properly the topic of this chapter. If all substances are capable of feeling, "material substance" cannot exist.

When Descartes sets out to investigate the nature of substance he finds that it is possible to be mistaken about all the deliverances of sense experience, but the actual experiencing or feeling is itself indubitable. "But it will be said that these phenomena are false and that I am dreaming. Let it be so; still it is at least quite certain that it seems to me that I see light, that I hear noise, and that I feel heat. That cannot be false; properly speaking, it is what is in me called feeling."[1] No reference to God is required to establish the existence of sentient substance. To be sure, Descartes loads his argument with the notion of the absolute identity of the "I," but he is very much aware that God is required to guarantee the validity of this addition. The important point is that Descartes' only assurance of the existence of material substance comes from his belief that God has created a world of absolute extension which corresponds more or less with the visual character of his perceptions. He has no arguments for the existence of material substance other than his faith that it exists and that God stands behind this faith.

The other men of the century, with the exception of Leibniz, followed Descartes. They asserted their belief in the existence of a dead material world,

[1] R. Descartes, *Works*, I, 153.

although Locke in his best moments states that this world is utterly unknowable. It remained for Berkeley to show that the supposition of extended substances was essentially meaningless. Now it is often supposed that the strength of Berkeley's argument follows from his definition, namely, "to be is to be perceived." Given this definition we may conclude that the existence of an unperceived material substance is contradictory. Many critics of Berkeley have pointed out this fact, apparently proceeding on the principle that in showing how Berkeley's argument followed from a definition they were not required themselves to clarify what they meant by the existence of unperceived material substance. It seems clear to me that the doctrine *esse est percipi* is not an important part of Berkeley's argument, since he asserts and defends his right to assert the existence of all sorts of things which he does not perceive. The point of the *esse est percipi* is that certain characters exist only as perceived. God is not perceived, yet God exists; and the same thing is true concerning other spiritual substances.[1]

To return once more, and for the last time in this chapter, to Hume, we can discover how much of Hume's attack on the notion of causal efficacy stemmed from the fact that he held an implicit belief in the existence of material substance. In his chapter on power he refers to and makes use of the Cartesian definition of matter to show the inconceivability of efficacy. And according to his own statement of procedure his investigation is restricted to a supposed observation of matter or "external bodies." Nor does

[1] Berkeley's argument and certain answers to it will be referred to again in more detail in the next chapter and in the Appendix.

he suppose that substance can have as a defining characteristic anything other than extension. When he explicitly discusses the question of substance he concludes rightly that the idea of substance cannot be derived from an impression of sensation, but he goes farther to the unwarranted conclusion that neither can it be derived from an impression of reflection. "I would fain ask those philosophers who found so much of their reasonings on the distinction of substance and accident, and imagine we have clear ideas of each, whether the idea of substance be derived from impressions of sensation or reflection? If it be conveyed to us by our senses, I ask, which of them and after what manner? If it be perceived by the eyes, it must be a colour; if by the ears, a sound; if by the palate, a taste; and so of the other senses. But I believe none will assert that substance is either colour or sound or taste. The idea of substance must therefore be derived from an impression of reflection, if it really exist. But the impressions of reflection resolve themselves into our passions and emotions; *none of which can possibly represent a substance*."[1] Leibniz says just what Hume tells us cannot possibly be said. He (Leibniz) secures his idea of substance from a consideration of the passions and emotions. It is regrettable that Hume's discussion of causation did not make use of the principle lying behind the above passage. Hume implies that anything seen through the eyes is a colour. What now is to be said of the "billiard-ball situation"? Hume could have added, if we derive our idea of cause from sight, then it must be a colour.

The answer to Hume is obvious. We infer the

[1] *Treatise*, I, 24. Italics mine.

actual nature of non-perceived entities and non-perceived relations, basing our inferences on direct impressions of reflection. In the billiard-ball situation we see only extended colour patches. We infer, however, the existence of events more or less like our own occasions of experience and having more or less the same relations. In any given case such an inference may be wrong. But this does not rob it of significance. Every term in the inference can have meaning drawn from our direct experience. It is not essential that we perceive the causal relation every time we assert its existence. What is essential is that we shall know what we mean when we make such assertions; and that the entities which are asserted to have such relations are not antecedently known to be unable to have them. Since then we may know what we mean by activity, and since we know nothing about substances or events which could make us suppose that such events or substances are incapable of influencing or being influenced by other events or substances, activity or efficacy can significantly be supposed to be a general character of causation.

CHAPTER VI

MATTER, CAUSATION, AND DETERMINISM

It is in considering the notion of matter that the significance of our definitions is completely established; for matter cannot be a cause, and yet the behaviour of matter is completely determined. According to Russell, "The two dogmas that constitute the essence of materialism are: first, the sole reality of matter; secondly, the reign of law."[1] The first dogma, namely, the assertion of the sole reality of matter, implies the denial of the reality of causation as we have defined it; the second, the assertion of the reign of law, implies a complete determinism. Russell explains the "reign of law" as implying "a belief in physical determinism, i.e. a belief that what happens in the world dealt with by physics happens according to laws such that, if we knew the whole state of the physical world during a finite time, however short, we could theoretically infer its state at any earlier or later time."[2] The first dogma coupled with this explanation of the second means that physical determinism is identical with universal determinism.

In a previous chapter I attempted to show that a theory of universal determinism which is not grounded in an appeal to God's uniform ways of acting is essentially meaningless. I used, as an example of such a theory, Laplace's statement of determinism. But such a theory is often held even to-day because of the confusion of the concept of causation with that of

[1] F. Lange, *History of Materialism*, introduction, xii.   [2] Ibid., ix.

determinism. This confusion can be seen in an examination of what may be considered the root assertion of physical determinism, the first law of motion. This law holds that "a body will continue at rest or in a state of uniform motion in a straight line, except in so far as it is compelled to change that state by impressed forces." This is the law as stated by Newton, but in one form or another it was common stock-in-trade to the thinkers of the seventeenth century. What is meant by the phrase "compelled to change that state by impressed forces"? If the phrase means that the activity of one body influences or affects another body, the law contains an assertion of the reality of the causal relation as we have defined it. On the other hand, if the phrase means merely that bodies act uniformly in terms of certain laws so that certain movements necessarily follow certain other movements, the law contains an assertion of determinism but says nothing at all about causation. But if this last interpretation is accepted, the untenability of the law is immediately apparent. How can we know that the movement of one body will necessarily be followed by the movement of another? It is not enough here to say that we know this because we know the law to be true. How do we know the law to be true? It is clear that we have not observed all bodies nor measured their movements. If it is said now that we do not know the law to be true, but merely *believe* it to be true, we are involved in the difficulties pointed out in the last chapter. The law (on the interpretation we are now considering) states that the movement of the second body is a necessary consequence of the movement of the first, and the *belief* that something is necessary, i.e. the belief in determinism, is self-contradictory. The assertion of determinism implies the possession of certain knowledge or the knowledge that at least one entity (God) possesses such certain knowledge. In the latter case I know that determinism is true, not because I know everything that will ever occur, but because I know that there is a God who knows everything that will ever occur. The concept of determinism involves absolute foreknowledge, that is to say, knowledge which makes the opposite of what is known, inconceivable. Hence a belief in determinism really means that someone believes, and admits the possibility that he may be wrong, that he cannot be wrong. This contradiction is often overlooked, since determinism is stated as an "if . . . then" proposition: namely, it is believed that "if all the causes were known, all the effects would be known." Since all the causes are not known, the meaning of the "if . . . then" form escapes testing.

But let us grant that all the causes are known; then the assertion of determinism involves the assertion that all the effects are known. But what is meant by saying that all the effects are known? Either it means that the non-occurrence of the effects is inconceivable; or, if it does not, we cannot have such knowledge. Granting a knowledge of all the causes, the assertion of determinism involves an assertion of necessary connection. Hence a belief in determinism asserts and denies necessary connection and is contradictory. It asserts (1) the belief in the occurrence of certain effects, which belief may be false, and (2) the assertion that the non-occurrence of such effects is inconceivable, and hence that the belief cannot be false.

Russell realizes that a "belief" in determinism is a "belief" in necessary connection, but he does not point out the contradiction involved in such a belief. When he says that the belief in determinism is a "belief that what happens in the world dealt with by physics happens according to laws such that, if we knew the whole state of the physical world during a finite time, however short, we could theoretically infer its state at any earlier or later time," the contradiction is disguised in the "if . . . then" and in the term "theoretically." The term "theoretically" refers to the "if." Since we do not know the whole state of the physical world during any finite time, the supposition that any later or earlier state could be inferred is only theoretical. However, if we grant that the state of the world for any finite time is completely known, the belief in determinism asserts that any other state can be known absolutely and not theoretically. The use of the "if . . . then" makes it possible to symbolize this argument. The believer in determinism asserts, "if A, then B." We grant A. The believer in determinism must then hold that B *must* be granted. B, however, is a fact distinct from A. The existence of A without B is conceivable; hence the statement that B *must* exist is nonsense. But if A is granted, and if it is impossible to state that B *must* exist, the "if A, then B" is meaningless. It can only be made meaningful if we are willing to assert a necessary connection between two matters of fact; and since the notion of necessary connection between matters of fact can only be given meaning in terms of absolute foreknowledge, a belief in necessary connection or determinism is a belief in absolute foreknowledge. As I have said, a belief, which involves the possibility of error, in the impossibility of error, is self-contradictory.

It may be said that the formulation of the deterministic position as "if A . . . then B" is not correct. Russell's statement could perhaps better be symbolized as "if P (a law) is true and A exists, then B exists." There is a sense in which this doctrine is completely innocuous, and it may be the sense in which Russell holds it. If a law expressing contingent relationships is true, the existence of such relationships may be deduced from the truth of the law; that is to say, given A and the known truth of the law that A stands in a certain relation to B, then the existence of this relation is necessary. Further, if we believe in the truth of the law, then we necessarily believe in what the law asserts. In the above criticism of Russell's statement I have assumed that Russell is presenting, not what he himself believes, but a historical doctrine, and the determinists we have considered meant to assert nothing as innocent as the above truism. Rather they meant to assert that the state of the world at any one time, which state might or might not be described by laws, necessitated some future state of the world, and this independently of any formulation of laws.[1]

[1] Consider, for example, Broad's definition of determinism: "Determinism is the name given to the following doctrine. Let s be any substance, ψ any characteristic, and t any moment. Suppose s is in fact in the state σ with respect to ψ at t. Then the compound supposition that everything else in the world should have been exactly as it in fact was *and* that s should instead have been in one of the other two alternative states with respect to ψ [i.e. different in any degree] is an impossible one." *Indeterminancy and Indeterminism*, Aristotelian Society, Supplementary Volume X, p. 136.

Broad not only defines determinism in this way, but he believes that it is a sensible doctrine, and that one could hold it and give significant reasons for holding it. Commenting on the above doctrine of determinism, Braithwaite says: ". . . I know *a priori* that his 'indeterminism' is true,

MATTER, CAUSATION, AND DETERMINISM

The first law of motion cannot then be interpreted as implying determinism, since we could never know that any body could determine any other body. But if we select the other proposed interpretation, we find other difficulties. If we suppose that the first law of motion asserts merely a causal relation between bodies, what is the nature of this causal relation? What is meant by the phrase "compelled to change by impressed forces"? In order to give this phrase meaning matter must be understood as capable of impressing forces upon other bits of matter and of receiving the impression of such forces. That is, we must give an intelligible account of how one bit of matter can influence another.

Here all depends upon the definition of matter, since from the definition various consequences as to the possibility of causal action follow. These consequences were recognized and admirably summed up by Hume. "For some of them, as the Cartesians in particular, having established it as a principle that we are perfectly acquainted with the essence of matter, have very naturally inferred that it is endowed with no efficacy, and that it is impossible for it of itself to communicate motion, or produce any of those effects which we ascribe to it. As the essence of matter consists in extension, and as extension implies not actual motion, but only mobility; they conclude that the energy which produced the motion cannot lie hid in the extension.

"This conclusion leads them into another, which

and true not only of one substance, one characteristic and one time, but of all substances, nearly all characteristics and all times." Ibid., p. 185. And Braithwaite would hold that the opposite of what is known *a priori* is either meaningless or self-contradictory.

they regard as perfectly unavoidable. Matter, say they, is in itself entirely unactive and deprived of any power by which it may produce, or continue, or communicate motion: but since these effects are evident to our sense, and since the power that produces them must be placed somewhere, it must lie in the Deity, or that divine being who contains in his nature all excellency and perfection. It is the Deity, therefore, who is the prime mover of the universe, and who not only first created matter, and gave it its original impulse, but likewise, by a continuous exertion of omnipotence, supports its existence, and successively bestows on it all those motions and configurations and qualities with which it is endowed."[1] If we consider the universe of matter by itself and without reference to God, we do not find efficacy or power in such a world.[2] It follows that if the idea of efficacy or power is not derivable from a consideration of matter, no meaning can be given to the phrase "compelled to change its state by impressed forces."[3]

[1] *Treatise*, I, 157.

[2] Hume argues against the Cartesians that the resource to God's omnipotence does not supply us with any idea of efficacy, since all ideas are derived from impressions and there is no impression of God's efficacy (Ibid., I, 158). However, Hume recognizes that this failure to find an "impression" of God's efficacy does not detract from the validity of the assertion of determinism based upon the knowledge of God's omnipotence: "The same imperfection attends our ideas of the Deity; but this can have no effect either on religion or morals. The order of the universe proves an omnipotent mind; that is, a mind whose will is *constantly attended* with the obedience of every creature and being. Nothing more is requisite to give a foundation to all the articles of religion; nor is it necessary we should form a distinct idea of the force and energy of the Supreme Being." Ibid., I, 159 n., italics Hume's.

[3] Reference to the Deity permits us to interpret the phrase in terms of determinism, but even such reference does not make intelligible an interpretation in terms of efficacy. See previous note.

In the last chapter it was made clear that the only thing which stands in the way of an activity view of causation is the belief in the existence of substances incapable of acting. Material substance, as it was defined by Descartes, for example, could be determined to movement, but it could not be the *cause* of movement. The term matter may of course be employed by those who regard matter as capable of acting and of transmitting energy or influence from one portion to another. Thus Russell, who holds that matter is a complex structure of events, finds that: "All genuine causal relations between different bodies involve this process of sudden loss of energy by one body and its sudden acquisition later by another body. The older physical laws, as reinterpreted by relativity, can apparently be so stated as to leave bodies independent of each other; but I cannot see how the quantum laws can be so stated."[1] And again: "I come now to what I call 'transactions' by which I mean quantum changes. I call them 'transactions' because energy is exchanged between different processes. We shall, then, hold that all causal relations consist of a series of rhythms or steady events separated by 'transactions.'"[2] Russell places quotation marks about the term "transactions," since as a physicist he is interested only in the formal properties of such transactions and the mathematical correlation of such properties. But when he leaves the treatment of these formal properties to discuss the "stuff" of the world he says, ". . . the theory of the foregoing pages has certain affinities with idealism—namely, that mental events are part of that stuff, and that the rest of the stuff resembles them more than it

[1] *Analysis of Matter*, 331.   [2] Ibid., 368.

resembles traditional billiard balls."[1] Broad has told us that "other grounds"[2] are required if we are to assert that all substances possess minds, and that we must assert this if we are to hold the activity view of causation. I take him to mean that we cannot *because* of being convinced of the truth of the activity view *therefore* assert that all substances possess minds, or are mental, or, as I have suggested, as the only requirement, are sentient. Rather on "other grounds" we must infer such mentalism or animism and go from there to the truth of the activity view. Mr. Russell goes a long way toward providing these "other grounds" in the passage quoted above.

Two questions remain to be answered in this chapter: (1) we must discover whether or not the addition of the concepts of "solidity" and "impenetrability" to the concept of extension enables us to regard matter as a cause; and (2) we must examine the arguments for the existence of matter as traditionally defined, that is, as sheer extension, or as extension plus solidity, impenetrability, and passivity.

The Cartesian doctrine of matter, as reviewed by Hume,[3] has already been stated. Descartes himself is agreeably explicit in the following: "That the nature of body consists not in weight, nor in hardness, nor in colour and so on, but in extension alone. In this way we shall ascertain that the nature of matter or of body in its universal aspect does not consist in its being hard or heavy or coloured, or that which affects our senses in some way, but *solely* in the fact that it is a substance extended in length, breadth, and depth."[4]

---

[1] *Analysis of Matter*, 388.   [2] Cf. page 177.   [3] *Treatise*, I, 157.
[4] R. Descartes, *Works*, I, *Principles*, Pt. II, princ. 4, 255–6.

The identification of space and body means not only that all extension is body, but that a body is merely a region of space. Although it is true that a region of space may have geometrical relations with other regions of space (as "bodies" may have geometrical relations), it is difficult to see what can be meant by the movement of a region of space (and "bodies" are supposedly movable). And even if we gloss over this difficulty, what meaning can we give to impenetrability as a quality of a "region of space?" "There is nothing in the formal determination of space to prevent any number of identically determinate modes [bodies] from co-existing in the same space. . . . But one 'body' excludes the simultaneous presence of any other from the same place. The possibility of any number of coincident figures co-existing in the same place is presupposed in all arguments by congruence of properties in geometry, and this is enough to show that the Cartesian reduction of matter to geometrical space precludes genuine individuality on the part of modes of matter ['bodies']."[1] But if regions of space are penetrable, that is, if two or more bodies can co-exist within the same dimensions, how is it possible to understand the action of one body upon another? What will prevent one body from moving directly through any body that it happens to meet in the path of its movement?

It should be further apparent that if Descartes meant by "body" merely extension in three dimensions, his quarrel with the atomists and the later quarrel of Newtonians and Cartesians was a quibble about the use of terms. No atomist or Newtonian would have

[1] S. V. Keeling, *Descartes*, 253, note.

denied that an atom was surrounded by extension. Whether or not we call this "extension in three dimensions" matter or void is of no importance so long as matter or void are conceived to have completely identical properties, namely, extension in three dimensions. That Descartes, however, thought it of great importance seems clear from his conclusion that the existence of a vacuum is inconceivable. "*That a vacuum or space in which there is absolutely no body is repugnant to reason*. With regard to a vacuum, in the philosophic sense of the term, that is, a space in which there is no substance, it is evident that such does not exist, seeing the extension of space of internal place is not different from that of body. For since from this alone, that a body has extension in length, breadth and depth, we have reason to conclude that it is a substance, it being absolutely contradictory that nothing should possess extension, we ought to form a similar inference regarding the space which is supposed void, viz. that since there is extension in it there is necessarily also substance."[1] Descartes is here denying in effect, if not in intent, the conceivability of the existence of body as he has defined body, i.e. as extension in three dimensions and *nothing else*. Body is not something distinct from extension. It is "that" which is extended, and the "that" does not refer here to a substance which has any other quality, or meaning, or claim to reality. So that when Descartes affirms the existence of body he is affirming the existence of a vacuum, and when he denies the existence of a vacuum he is denying the existence of body.

Since Descartes both asserted the existence of body

[1] *Works*, I, *Principles*, Pt. II, princ. 16, 185.

and denied the existence of a vacuum (and meant by "body" and "vacuum" the same thing), his notion of the existence of material substance appears to be self-contradictory, and thus meaningless. There are, however, several different interpretations in terms of which we may attempt to resolve this contradiction. On the first interpretation we suppose Descartes to be expressing his preference for a term. He likes the term "body," but he does not like the term "vacuum." Hence he declares that a vacuum does not exist, although he already has affirmed the existence of a vacuum under the name "body." I hold this interpretation to be unsatisfactory, since it can be shown that Descartes retained an undeclared and undefined notion of impenetrability. The Cartesian material substance then becomes an impenetrable substance extended in three dimensions. In this case, since body is defined independently of extension, Descartes may significantly deny the existence of extended nothing. But this interpretation gets us into difficulties if we attempt to make it consistent with other statements of Descartes. We have clear and distinct ideas of extension, but no clear and distinct ideas of "impenetrable substance." Since we can only affirm the existence of that of which we have a clear and distinct idea, we cannot affirm the existence of "impenetrable substance" or of material substance having an essence not exhausted in the character of being extended in three dimensions.

It may be said finally that all this has been a useless bother, since Descartes was interested solely in the geometric properties of matter. So far as he is, he says nothing about the *existence* of matter. And so far as he says nothing about the *existence* of matter, what he says about its geometric properties is of no consequence to a doctrine of causation.

My conclusion here can best be expressed in a hypothetical proposition. If we are to make sense of Descartes' denial of a vacuum and of his arguments against action at a distance, we must for these purposes at least suppose Descartes to have held a view of material substance as extended *and* impenetrable. Whether he did or not I cannot say. I presume that he did whenever he discussed a vacuum or action at a distance, since I should suppose he wanted to make sense of these discussions. And, of course, that he didn't whenever he said that "body consists in extension alone" and that our clear and distinct idea of matter is the idea of extension. I have before this attempted to show why Descartes must hold that matter is more than extension when he denies the existence of a vacuum. Why must he hold such a view when he discusses action at a distance? Because of this: The Cartesians argued that no body could influence another body through a void, and hence that the movements of the heavenly bodies must be explained by the movement of contiguous bodies. But if by body Descartes meant sheer extension, the controversy loses its point, since no Newtonian ever denied that "extension" was contiguous to all heavenly bodies. If there is any significant argument, it must be as to whether or not the "contiguous extension" is the property of a substance which has properties other than extension, namely, solidity and impenetrability. Unless there are such bodies which *ex hypothesi* transmit motion to one another, Descartes' whole system of mechanics must be regarded as based on the notion of action at a distance or action through the void. When the Cartesians argue that movement must be transmitted through contiguous bodies, if what is meant by body is merely extension, the Newtonians can reply that gravity acts through contiguous bodies (space or extension).

Locke employs this notion of solidity or impenetrability to distinguish space from body. "*On solidity depends resistance, impulse, and protrusion.* By this idea of solidity is the extension of body distinguished from the extension of space: that extension of body being nothing but the cohesions or continuity of solid, separable, movable parts; and the extension of space, the continuity of unsolid, inseparable, and immovable parts. Upon the solidity of bodies also depend their mutual impulse, resistance, and protrusion. . . . *What it* [*solidity*] *is*. If anyone asks me what this solidity is, I send him to his senses to inform him: let him put a flint or a football between his hands, and then endeavour to join them, and he will know . . ."[1] He also in the opening line of this passage seems to assert that the notion of solidity explains the "action" of matter. (See first question, page 200.) But an examination of the second part of the passage should convince us that Locke has mistaken the direction of dependence in the opening line. He recognizes that our idea of solidity ("what it is") depends on the *feeling* of pressure and resistance. What solidity is independently of the feeling of resistance must remain a mystery. Through the use of the notion of solidity we can perhaps explain the causal action of matter.

[1] *Essay*, 78–9.

But this means that we must suppose matter to *feel* resistance and to exert pressure, since the idea of solidity arises from such feelings. The attempt to define solidity or impenetrability in divorce from feelings leads to the assertion of the existence of an *ad hoc* "occult quality." We say that if one body strikes another it will be deflected from its course, or "compelled to change its course by impressed forces"; then if we ask for the meaning of this compulsion or why it will be deflected from its course, we are told that the body is impenetrable or solid; if now we ask what it means for a body to be solid and impenetrable, and are told that it means that a body that strikes another will be deflected or "compelled to change, etc.," we have indeed gained precious information. We know as much as the man who explained that "opium produces sleep because of its dormative qualities." To say now that what is meant by the deflection is merely that the movement of one body follows another is to admit that no idea of causation can be derived from a consideration of matter. And this brings us to our final decision as to the first possible interpretation of the phrase "compelled to change by impressed forces."[1] The phrase can have no meaning if it is understood to refer to bits of matter.[2]

I realize that any discussion of the first law of motion, and consequently this one, is open to the charge of exorcizing ghosts when we no longer believe in their existence. But I believe that the consideration

---

[1] See page 193.

[2] This repeats the conclusion given on page 198. There, however, the scope of the conclusion was restricted to the Cartesian doctrine of matter as reproduced by Hume. The conclusion here is more general, since it is reached after a consideration of matter as "solid" as well as extended.

I have given to the possible meanings of the law illustrates the confusion between the terms "cause" and "determine." By confusion I do not mean that the two notions are identified. I mean that sleight-of-hand substitution of one notion for the other is used to disguise the nonsense of materialism; that is, to disguise the fact that the two dogmas of materialism taken together do not make sense. If the dogma affirming universal determinism is examined, it can easily be shown that it involves the assertion of necessary connection and cannot be maintained consistently with the first dogma which denies the existence of God (by implication). If, however, the materialist holds that contrary to Russell's interpretation he means by the "reign of law" only that the entities that constitute the world are *causally* connected, what of the other dogma? If matter is the sole reality, it is impossible to find a meaning for the term cause or efficacy. In this predicament the materialist becomes a positivist or sceptic, and asserts only that the movement of one particle of matter follows the movement of another. This means, in effect, that the dogma of determinism is given up and that the dogma of the sole reality of matter is implicitly retained. Otherwise how can we explain the constant assertion that efficacy or power is incomprehensible?[1]

---

[1] Hume, the founder of modern positivism and so-called "empiricism," ruthlessly deletes our experience of any impression of efficacy or power: "Or if they esteem that opinion absurd and impious, as it really is, I shall tell them how they may avoid it; and that is, by concluding from the very first that they have no idea of power or efficacy in any object; since neither in body nor spirit, neither in superior nor inferior natures are they able to discover one single instance of it. . . . All ideas are derived from and represent impressions. We never have any impression that contains power or efficacy. We never, therefore, have any idea of power." *Treatise*, I, 158–9.

I return now to the second question asked above, namely, what reason have we for believing in the reality of matter? I do not say "sole reality of matter," because I believe that such a dogma requires no attack; it cannot be intelligently maintained.[1] The question concerns not the existence of something to which we give the name matter, but the existence of something defined as extended, solid, and passive. The terms "solid" and "extended" are the traditional terms used to describe the "billiard balls" which compose the physical world. The term "passive" requires some explanation. I stated at the opening of this chapter that the behaviour of matter has been traditionally understood as being completely determined. So long as God's causality remains an integral element in scientific explanation, the entities which constitute the physical world must be understood as completely passive; that is, what happens in the world must follow absolutely from God's power. Hence, all finite powers are eliminated.

The concept of quiescent mass or complete passivity was contained in the concept of matter during the seventeenth century. It is implied in the denial of occult qualities. The "matter" of the early Greek philosophers was animate and alive;[2] the atoms of Lucretius had a spontaneous power of movement;[3] the cabalists of the Middle Ages believed that all matter was alive and endowed with energy and power;

---

[1] There can be no empirical argument for the "sole reality of matter." The very fact of experience means that something exists capable of experiencing or feeling.

[2] W. Windelband, *History of Philosophy*, 32; E. Zeller, *Outlines of the History of Greek Philosophy*, 25.

[3] Lucretius, *De Rerum Natura*, Munro's translation, 49-51.

during the fifteenth and sixteenth centuries Leonardo, Campanella, Bruno and others affirmed the living quality of the world;[1] at the opening of the seventeenth century, Bacon talked of matter as "perceiving";[2] and Gilbert held that the earth had a soul.[3] Even during the seventeenth century Newton spoke of "subtle spirits lying hid in all matter"; Leibniz concluded that all monads perceived; and we find Spinoza saying that all things are animate.[4] Yet in spite, or perhaps because, of this imposing historical background, the thinkers of the seventeenth century did formulate a conception of matter from which all notions of power, life, efficacy, and force were eliminated, or, as they chose to put it, they denied the existence of all occult qualities (efficient causes).

One cannot explain this change of heart and consequent denial of occult causes on the ground that such causes are not perceived, for neither is dead matter perceived. Descartes, who perhaps more than any other single individual is responsible for our modern common-sense notion of matter, asserted its existence not because he perceived it, but because he had an innate idea of such matter which was clear and distinct. No one has ever perceived "atoms" nor has anyone ever perceived sheer undifferentiated extension. There are undoubtedly elements of our experience which are hypostatized to form the conception of matter; but the question is, why certain of these elements and not others? We do not see the feelings of matter; but

---

[1] H. O. Taylor, *Thought and Expression in the Sixteenth Century*, II, xxx, sect. 3, xxxi, xxxiv, sect. 1.

[2] *Silva Silvarum*, sect. 9.

[3] W. Gilbert, *On the Loadstone and Magnetic Bodies*, Motteley translation.

[4] *Ethics*, Pt. 2, prop. 13, note.

neither do we "see" our own, nor those of another human being.

Descartes meant by a clear and distinct idea any idea from which certain consequences could immediately be deduced. Hence, he asserted that he had clear and distinct ideas of extension, because of the deductive character of geometry. He saw also that deductive knowledge about matter of fact required that the sequence of events be deducible from known laws regarded as statements of God's uniform manner of acting. It is obvious that the existence of occult causes would make such deductive knowledge impossible. God could not be the sole cause nor could His laws be absolute, if lurking in finite things there were powers and energy which at any moment might upset the deterministic scheme. Hence the entities which follow God's laws must be conceived as completely passive and amenable to absolute determinism. The existence of souls, of course, gives Descartes moments of difficulty. To avoid them Descartes found it necessary not only to deny occult qualities but to establish a break between the physical world and the world of spirits. But the important point is that Descartes regarded the physical world as composed of entities whose behaviour is completely determined, that is to say, the *physical* world was, for him, composed of matter defined as completely determined.

It can now be shown that the two dogmas of materialism are internally related provided that the dogma of the sole reality of matter is modified to except the reality of God. The reality of God (as omniscient and omnipotent) insures the truth of the dogma of determinism and the dogma of the sole reality of matter (God's reality being excepted) follows as a consequence.[1] I concluded above that if the dogma of determinism is given up and the dogma of the sole reality of matter is retained, the only relation between bodies can be one of succession. But now it has been shown that the assertion of the existence of entities incapable of causal action is one of the consequences of the assertion of determinism. Matter denotes something passive, something completely determined; so the sole reality of matter implies the truth of determinism. If we wish to assert the truth of the antecedent without asserting the truth of the consequent, we must discover a new meaning for the term matter, that is to say, the character of passivity or of being completely determined must be eliminated. Hence the question as to whether the entities which constitute the physical world are capable of *action* must remain open.

But the possibility of action, which results from recognizing that the character of complete passivity cannot be maintained independently of the dogma of determinism, is not enough. The two remaining traditional characters of matter, namely, solidity and extension, do not seem to provide for the existence of this possibility. In other words, when we eliminate determinism, we establish merely the possibility of efficient causes. But if an empirical examination of the existential world discloses that the entities which constitute the physical world can be exhaustively described in terms of extension and solidity, the meaning of causation which has been established is not applicable to the physical world, although it may be applicable

[1] I am here considering matter defined merely as passive.

to the world of sentient entities. Hence we must examine the arguments for the belief in the existence of matter, as defined by the two remaining qualities, extension and solidity.

In the first place, it should be clear that no attempt is to be made to deny or impugn the experience of extension or resistance. The materialist does not assert merely that we experience such qualities, but that these qualities define the nature of substances or realities which exist independently of our perception. When we restrict our discussion of this point to philosophers of the seventeenth century, we find the refutation of materialism very simple. Indeed the untenability of materialism was clearly realized and demonstrated by Leibniz. I shall consider Leibniz's criticism after considering the arguments against which they were directed. How completely these latter arguments have been misunderstood is shown if we consider Lange's statement that "Lamettrie took a malicious delight in giving himself out as a Cartesian, and affirming, perhaps in good faith, that Descartes had explained man on mechanical principles, and had only attached a soul to a machine to please the parsons."[1] It may be that Descartes did try to "please the parsons," but if the parsons are wrong in their belief in God, Descartes has not even the fraction of a reason to assert the existence of anything like a machine. To be sure, he tells us he perceives extension and feels resistance; but without a recourse to the goodness and veracity of God, there is no ground upon which he can assert the existence of material substance. If Lamettrie wishes to dispense with the parsons and

[1] F. Lange, *History of Materialism*, II, 111.

still consider himself a Cartesian, he must also dispense with the belief in the existence of material substance.

However much we may dislike parsons, and however poor we may think Descartes' resort to the goodness and veracity of God, at least if we grant that the parsons are right, Descartes' argument appears intelligible. But if we consider the arguments by which Hobbes tried to prove the existence of bodies (independently of any appeal to God) we must leave the realm of intelligible discourse. Hobbes begins his discussion with a definition of space as a phantasm which exists only in the mind. He then defines body as something which is contained in some part of space and yet exists independently of the mind. In an endeavour to make sense out of this notion one commentator[1] has said that Hobbes confuses three kinds of space—psychological, epistemological, and physical space. There could only be a confusion between such spaces if there were such spaces. A simpler and more adequate explanation is the view that Hobbes said contradictory things about the same character, namely, extension. For myself, I see no way of understanding how the contents of that which is "in the mind" can be "out of the mind." I do not think the difficulty here is merely one of distinguishing between awareness and that of which one is aware, as Moore holds in the *Refutation of Idealism*. I shall return to this distinction in a later discussion of Moore's argument.

I find it almost impossible to obtain from the writings of Locke a clear account of material substance. Early in the *Essay* he makes the traditional distinction

[1] F. Brandt, *Thomas Hobbes' Mechanical Conception of Nature*, Chap. viii, 250.

between primary and secondary qualities; but later the force of his own logic leads him to the recognition that our ideas of substance are nothing but collections of simple ideas: "I say, our specific ideas of substances are nothing else but a collection of a certain number of simple ideas, considered as united into one thing. These ideas of substances, though they are commonly called 'simple apprehensions,' and the names of them 'simple terms,' yet, in effect, are complex and compounded."[1] And since he says that "Whatsoever the mind perceives *in itself*, or is the immediate object of perception, thought, or understanding I call idea,"[2] it is difficult to determine what he could have meant by material substance. It seems clear from these last passages that he could not have meant a substance existing external to the mind or perception. Yet his distinction between primary and secondary qualities seems to mean just that. But, as I have said, his own analysis leads him to the conclusion that the primary qualities are ideas in the mind on the same footing as the secondary qualities; both are ideas which the "mind perceives in itself." To say that the nature of external substance consists in extension and solidity, aside from the difficulty of explaining how matter so defined could produce anything (a difficulty of which Locke himself was fully aware) involves us in the difficulty of understanding how a collection of ideas in the mind could acquire external existence. Hence the conclusion that external substance is unknowable. Whatever knowledge we have of external existence, Locke supposes, is gained through the senses, but this knowledge is only that "something" exists which

[1] *Essay*, 216.   [2] Ibid., 85.

has the *power* to affect our senses.[1] In a previous chapter I have mentioned Locke's belief that "Powers make a large part of our complex ideas of substances," and that "material substance is devoid of power." It would seem to follow that the external substance which has the power to affect our senses cannot be "matter."[2] Again the point might be made that Locke's difficulty with the notion of material substance rests in confusing the act of perception with what is perceived. This argument is used by Moore against Berkeley whose denial of the existence of material substance was more careful and consistent than was that of Locke.

Berkeley's argument has been briefly considered in the previous chapter. Berkeley did not deny the existence of "external" substances; he denied merely the existence of external material substance. And the root of his denial is the recognition that the correspondence theory of perception, which he repudiated, and the causal theory of perception, which he accepted, have nothing to do with one another. Although I did not explicitly mention the causal theory of perception, it was involved in my conclusion that the direct perception of extension and succession is not direct perception of material bodies existing independently of the act of perception. I may say here that most attempts to present a consistent theory of perception seem to me to fail because of a failure to distinguish between the causal theory and the correspondence

---

[1] *Essay*, 537.

[2] It should be remembered that the idea of power is not, for Locke, an idea of sensation, and the difficulty he finds with the *locus* of the primary and secondary qualities does not concern the idea of power.

theory of perception.[1] I take it that the frequent assertions in text-books and histories to the effect that Berkeley was a solipsist or a phenomenalist are due to the failure to realize the distinction between the causal and the correspondence theory of perception; for Berkeley frequently asserts the existence of other substances.

The causal theory of perception asserts that our perceptions are caused by something external to the perception. The correspondence theory of perception asserts that what causes our perception is identical with what we perceive. So far as the secondary qualities were concerned, Descartes and Locke realized quite clearly that it was not necessary that the cause of our idea of such qualities possess such qualities; but as for the primary qualities, they supposed that the qualities of the cause corresponded exactly to the perceived quality. Berkeley never denied that what we perceive is caused by something external; but decidedly thought it nonsense to say that a perception of extension is caused by extension when we mean by that statement to assert the existence of two extensions identical in all respects. I take Berkeley's argument to be directed against this duplication of primary qualities. Primary and secondary qualities are alike for him in being effects of external substances, and there is no more reason to suppose that what is external is in itself extended or corresponds to the extended character of a visual field than that it is sour or valuable. A causal theory of perception says only

[1] One of the latest of these attempts, for example, finds the causal theory untenable by attacking the correspondence theory. H. H. Price, *Perception*, Chap. iv.

MATTER, CAUSATION, AND DETERMINISM

that our perceptions are caused; it says, in itself, nothing about the nature of the cause.

Moore's argument against Berkeley cuts across the causal theory and the correspondence theory of perception. He holds that Berkeley asserts that what exists, exists only as it is perceived. He argues from this that since that object perceived is distinct from the act of perception, it is impossible to assert a necessary connection between them and, therefore, that there is nothing contradictory or inconceivable about the existence of the object apart from the act of perception. This argument is plausible only so long as the term "existence" is given no meaning. Berkeley does not deny that other entities which he does not perceive exist; he denies merely that material substance exists. Hence Moore must show, if he wishes to refute Berkeley, that what exists independently of an act of perception is material substance, and not some "X." For Berkeley not only asserted that something external to his perception existed; he ascribed a character to that something, namely, he called it spiritual substance. Divorced from its religious implications this is the assertion of the external existence of sentient substance. If Moore's argument is to have any significance as directed against Berkeley, he must show that what exists external to any perception is not spiritual substance but material substance. He seems to be doing just that when he asserts the independent *existence* of objects of perception (which, *prima facie*, do not seem sentient), because he leaves the term existence without any meaning. If we attempt to give the term "existence" a fixed meaning, his argument collapses. Consider Moore's own example of the "awareness of blue."

What is meant by saying that the "blue" may exist independently of the "awareness" of it? If we mean that there may exist other cases of "awareness of blue," we say nothing excluded by Berkeley's conclusion. What it must mean is that the proposition "the blue exists" is significant without reference to any perceiver. There is, so far as I know, but one traditional method of attempting to give such a proposition meaning in divorce from an act of perception. And that is by saying that the blue qualifies a material substance or exists in space and time. But this implies that "existence" means "occupation of a region of space and time." It thus becomes important to say what we mean by space and time. If by space and time we mean what Hobbes meant by space and time (something existing only in the mind) we have secured the independent existence of the blue by locating it in the mind. In this case the argument proves the reverse of what it was designed to prove. Can this conclusion be avoided if the independent existence of space and time is asserted? What, then, do we mean by the existence of space? The only consistent reply is that "space exists" means "space occupies space." I take this to be nonsense, and I conclude that it is impossible to answer Berkeley by defining existence in terms of location in space, since his question has already gone beyond such an answer. He wishes to know what is meant by the external (independent) existence of extension or space itself. Again, I should like to say that this difficulty with the notion of external substance seems to me peculiar to materialism. There is no difficulty in asserting the external existence of other perceptions or systems of perceptions. Thus

Berkeley can say that the cause of his perceptions is external spiritual substance. In any given case, when the existence of such a cause is asserted, the assertion has meaning. I know what is meant by the existence of external sentient substance. I mean that there *are* other perceptions external to (existing independently of) my own; and by the real world I mean the system of perceptions.[1]

This seems to me the conclusion of Leibniz. In a brief autobiography of intellectual development,[2] Leibniz tells us that though he was originally an atomist, he came to recognize that materialism had merely imaginative or pictorial advantages and could not be intelligently maintained. Thus in his final view he regarded extension not as the character of substance but as an order of co-existing substances. Leibniz's difficulty in correlating this order with the actual perception of extension is due to the windowless character of the monads. He found it necessary to account for the perception of the order in terms of a pre-established harmony. In the doctrine of the causal relations of perceptions or events which I have advanced we do not find such a difficulty. Extendedness becomes in this doctrine the mode of togetherness within a perception. The character of extension arises from the community of many perceptions in the causal ancestry of the perception so qualified.

It is unimportant for my purposes to work out the positive implications of this notion of extension. It has been attempted by Bergson in various works, and

---

[1] I have added a further discussion of the relation of Berkeley and Moore in an Appendix.
[2] Leibniz, *The Monadology and Other Philosophical Writings*, 352.

accomplished by Whitehead in *Process and Reality*. The purpose of this investigation is not to discuss the manner in which the perception of extension or togetherness arises, but to exhibit the untenability of the assertion of the independent existence of matter. I have concentrated my efforts on the character of extension; but the same type of examination would, I think, disclose the impossibility of regarding "solidity" as existing independently of any act of perception.

A last word might be said about the agreement of the doctrine presented here with what modern physicists tell us about the physical world. "The science of physics conceives a natural occasion as a locus of energy. Whatever else that occasion may be, it is an individual fact harbouring that energy. The words electron, proton, photon, wave motion, velocity, hard and soft radiation, chemical elements, matter, empty spaces, temperature, degradation of energy, all point to the fact that physical science recognizes qualitative differences between occasions in respect to the way in which each occasion entertains its energy.

"These differences are entirely constituted by the flux of energy, that is to say, by the way in which the occasions in question have inherited their energy from the past of nature and in which they are about to transmit their energy to the future."[1] Here the term energy is used abstractly and the real entities involved are given the name of occasions ("occasions of experience"). "An occasion of experience which includes a human mentality is an extreme instance at one end of the scale, of those happenings which constitute nature."[2]

[1] A. N. Whitehead, *Adventures of Ideas*, 237-8.   [2] Ibid., 237.

The contemporary philosophic temper can best be indicated by noting that the view here articulated will probably be criticized as "animistic." Such a criticism seems to me significant only if it is backed by a materialistic alternative. When we have found, as I think I have found, that we have no good reasons for a belief in dead material substance, what argument remains against the view that feeling is the defining characteristic of substance? This does not mean that every substance can think or is conscious. "For those things which we have so far propounded have been altogether general, and have not appertained more to man than to other individual things which are all, though in various grades, animate."[1]

[1] Spinoza, *Ethics*, Pt. II, prop. 13, note.

CHAPTER VII

FREEDOM AND UNIFORMITY

PROPOSITIONS about necessary connection must be capable of demonstration; the "belief" in necessary connection is meaningless. Exactly why this is so has been explained in Chapter IV. When we assert that two entities are necessarily connected we assert nothing about any existential relation but only that it is possible to deduce the existence of one entity from the other. Any deduced conclusion involves the inconceivability of its opposite. Since the opposite of any existential situation is always conceivable, no matter-of-fact relation is necessary. A belief in necessary connection is a belief in the possibility of deducing matter-of-fact relations, and since it is nonsense to suppose that matter-of-fact relations can be deduced, it is nonsense to believe in necessary connection. As we have seen, this conclusion does not follow if an omnipotent, omniscient God is implicated in matter-of-fact relations.

When we come to consider propositions about freedom or causation, any question of demonstration is wholly irrelevant. That any entities are free or are causally related to other entities could not be demonstrated any more than it could be demonstrated that this paper is white. The concepts of causation and freedom refer to characters of matters of fact, to questions of existence; and questions of existence cannot be solved demonstratively.

There is a difficulty, however, which concerns propositions about freedom which results from the alleged doctrine that the denials of meaningless propositions are themselves meaningless.[1] If the denial of freedom implies the assertion of necessary connection and the assertion of necessary connection is nonsense, then the assertion of freedom is not a significant proposition. This difficulty is avoided if we recollect that the opposite of freedom is not necessary connection but passivity.[2] Throughout this essay I have employed the opposition of freedom and necessary connection, because the historical opposition was stated in these terms. Further, in order to assert the sole causality of God and the consequent necessity of all connections, it was first necessary to assert that all things are passive, that is to say, determined. In other words, the assertion of necessary connection implies that it is false that anything is free, but the meaning of freedom is not secured through the denial of necessary connection.

However, this chapter shall not be primarily concerned with assertions of freedom. The question whether or not anything is free seems to me to be capable of immediate answer in terms of direct introspection. A more important topic is the question of "degrees of freedom." The notion of degrees of freedom does not imply that there are degrees of determinism, since the notion of determinism admits of no variation in degree.

"Degrees of freedom" refers to the inheritance of causal influence from prior events. For certain purposes, especially when large systems or groups of events are being considered, the underived activity of individual events may be considered as negligible.

---

[1] I do not hold this doctrine.   [2] See Chapter I, p. 34.

The character of the group or system may then be described in terms of a common characteristic inherited by the system from the other events which constitute the environment. A more detailed treatment of the relation of freedom to causation will perhaps make this point clear. I take causation to refer to the transmission of energy, influence, or "subjective form" from one event to another. I take freedom to refer to the fact that the transmission follows from the activity of the event which is the cause. An event inherits various influences from the events which are its causal ancestors, but the organization of these influences and their transmission to subsequent events involves a degree of unique activity on the part of all events. It is the case that certain events possess to a marked degree the ability to modify inherited influences. In such cases we are sensible of what is usually called freedom, novelty, or contingency. In cases where the modification contributed by any individual event is negligible, we are more sensible of uniformity, permanence and order.

In amplifying what has just been said, I wish first to discuss certain prejudices which may afford points of departure for criticism of my view, and secondly, to remedy the abstraction of the above account by giving examples of the characteristics and relationships described. One of the prejudices is the interpretation of the causal relation in terms of what might be called the type event of materialism, i.e. of one bit of matter causing the movement of another or following the movement of another. Such a view no longer receives the support of physical science. "The traditional view, that physics is concerned exclusively with matter in motion, cannot be maintained for a number of reasons. In the first place, the aether, even if it can be said to exist, can hardly be regarded as having a granular structure, and events in it, such as the passage of light, cannot be explained as movements of particles of aether. In the second place, quantum changes, if they are really sudden, violate the continuity of motion, and thus destroy its advantages as an imaginative picture. In the third place—*and this is philosophically the most important point*—the conception of motion depends upon that of persistent material substances, which we have seen reason to regard as merely an approximate empirical generalization. Before we can say that one piece of matter has moved, we must decide that two events at different times belong to one 'biography,' and a 'biography' is defined by certain causal laws not by persistence of substance. Consequently motion is something constructed with the laws of physics, or—we might say—as a convenience in stating them; it cannot be one of the fundamental concepts of physics."[1] In this passage Russell is working from within the causal theory of perception. He admits that we perceive continuous motion or "material bodies," but holds that the motion, extension, and solidity which characterize material bodies are characters of perception and not characters of the external world.[2]

Russell sets off the term "biography" in quotation marks as he did the term "transaction." He does so

---

[1] B. Russell, *Analysis of Matter*, 355-6. Italics mine.
[2] Ibid., 385: "The wrong views as to physical space have been encouraged by the notion that the primary qualities are objective, which has been held imaginatively by many men who would have emphatically repudiated it so far as their explicit thought was concerned."

I think not only because of the novelty of the term, but because he realizes that physical science is not concerned with supplying content to such terms or conceptions. Physics, for Russell, is concerned with the formal properties of "biographies" and "transactions." The causal laws which he mentions are statements of these structural or formal properties. However, this account of formal or structural properties, although it may be the only problem of physics, does not exhaust the "philosophy of nature." No description of nature in terms of structure or formal properties can be regarded as complete. Hobson, who believes that natural science can dispense with the notion of efficient causation, just on this account believes that natural science requires to be supplemented with a philosophy of nature. "All that has been maintained in the earlier part of this lecture is that natural science, as distinct from a complete philosophy of nature, in the method it adopts of describing conceptually that part of our experience which we call physical, had no need of the conception of efficient causation and can make no use of it for its own special purposes. . . . It is just the absence of the conception of efficient causation . . . in the kind of account which natural science is able to give of portions of the world of physical phenomena that prevents us from regarding such account as explanatory in the strict sense of the term. Philosophy has always occupied itself with attempts to find explanations in the complete sense; and thus to condemn *a priori* as necessarily illusory, the notions of efficient causation, activity (and purposiveness), amounts to a dogmatic denial of all validity, and of all possibility of success to metaphysical thought. Some men of science are apparently prepared to take up this dogmatic attitude towards metaphysical philosophy. Their position, however, admits of no justification by arguments of demonstrative, or even cogent force. *It is in opposition to what is at least* prima facie *the most immediate knowledge we possess, that derived from the experience we have when we will and act.*[1] The view expressed by Hobson is very much like that expressed by Mach, when he declares that: "The science of mechanics does not comprise the foundations, no, nor even a part of the world, but only an aspect of it."[2] It is the view expressed by Leibniz, and by Russell, when they hold that spatial relations are abstract. There is, however, nothing vicious about a concern with abstractions. Difficulty arises only when we become guilty of what Whitehead has called "the fallacy of misplaced concretion," that is, when we substitute our abstractions for the concrete reality. However, "The mere phrase that 'physical science is an abstraction' is a confession of philosophical failure. It is the business of rational thought to describe the more concrete fact from which the abstraction is derivable."[3] The more concrete fact is, in every case, an occasion of experience; it is an event which involves activity and efficient causation. The scientific notion of uniformity is an abstraction derived from the community of subjective form shared by the concrete events which constitute nature.[4] These long quotations

---

[1] E. W. Hobson, *The Domain of Natural Science*, 86–7. Italics mine.
[2] E. Mach, *Science of Mechanics*, 307.
[3] A. N. Whitehead, *Adventures of Ideas*, 239.
[4] Whitehead has attempted to give an account of such derivation especially as it concerns the uniformities or relations of extensive connection.

are an attempt to show that "an appeal to physical science" cannot be made the ground for denying the truth of the account given above of causation and freedom. For the traditional "matter in motion," Russell proposes to substitute "periodic processes," "rhythms," and "transactions" as the types of physical occurrences.

If we wish to know more than the formal nature of occurrences, we must turn our attention from physics to that "immediate knowledge . . . derived from the experience we have when we will and act." I take it that act here does not refer to the "movement" of the body, since Hobson is giving us an account of efficient causation which for him is not a relation between bodies. Both movement and body have reality only as elements in perceptions or events.[1] "The immediate knowledge derived from the experience we have when we will and act" refers to the feeling of power and activity; it refers to our immediate perception (or simple idea) of the transition of efficacy or influence from one experience to another, that is to say, from one event to another. It is in considering these relationships that we gain insight into the concrete nature of events. Again I point out, that this view, although currently unfashionable, was stated in all essentials by Leibniz. The concrete fact for Leibniz is always a perception or an appetition. Perception and appetition are not to be confused with the "object

[1] "Whilst other English physicists were distracted by vortex-atoms and other will-o'-the-wisps, Clifford was convinced that these geometrical notions were only partial aspects of the relations of what he calls elements of feeling. 'The reality corresponding to our perception of matter is an element of the complex thing we call feeling . . .'" Eddington, *Space, Time and Gravitation*, 192. Reference is to W. K. Clifford, *Fortnightly Review*, 1875.

of perception or appetite." What is real is the perceiving, the activity, the appetite. Objects are partial aspects, elements abstracted from the concrete event. It is meaningless to suppose that the elements "exist" apart from the concrete event or perception. Moore, who, so far as I know, is the only man who has attempted to meet this view directly, admits ultimately that he cannot give any meaning to the term "existence."[1]

A full discussion of the nature of perceptions is the business of systematic metaphysics or philosophy. Such a discussion cannot be undertaken here. For my purposes it is only necessary to indicate those characters of experience to which we apply the terms causation and freedom. This has already been done in respect to causation. Freedom, as I have said, refers to the fact that causal influence inherited by any occasion of experience, is modified, more or less, by the inheriting occasion before the inheriting occasion becomes the cause of a subsequent occasion. Let us consider specifically the type of experience to which I have referred before. A moment of anger transmits its emotional tone to a subsequent experience. This subsequent experience is under no necessity of transmitting in its turn the emotional quality it has inherited, although in cases of sustained emotion something like this undoubtedly happens. But in other cases, which are more susceptible of introspection, introspection discloses that each occasion modifies the quality it inherits before transmitting it to later occasions.

Another illustration of this meaning of freedom can be found in an examination of the perennial quarrel

[1] G. E. Moore, *Philosophical Studies*, 78.

in the biological sciences between those who emphasize conditioning and the influence of the environment and those who emphasize inheritance. It is obvious that inheritance is but a highly specialized form of conditioning. No meaning can be given to "conditioning" unless we imply by it the inheritance by the organism of influences from the events which constitute its historical environment; and no meaning can be given to "inheritance" unless we imply by it the conditioning by such an environment. There is, however, an important issue hidden beneath this specialized nonsense (the quarrel between conditioning and inheritance). That issue concerns the degree to which any event or entity transforms the influences which it inherits. For the purposes of a special science it may be possible to regard a system of events as an organism. In this case we may distinguish between the free activity of the organism and the causal influence of the environment. But for philosophy, the distinction between organism and environment, as most biologists and psychologists use it, is superficial, though meaningful. Ultimately the events which constitute the organism are parts of the environment of any particular act or event. The environment, for example, of an act of perception is constituted by all the events which are its causal ancestors. Some of these events may compose the "body" of the organism.

We have little reason to believe that except in high-grade organisms there is any consciousness or awareness of transmitted feelings. Since it is a truism to assert that we know about our own feelings only when we are conscious of them, it may be objected that we can mean nothing by feeling divorced from consciousness. What, then, can be meant by using the term feeling as I have used it[1]—as the defining character of all real events, since I do not hold that all events involve consciousness? I should say, first, that it seems to me clear that our own experiences or feelings at least do not always involve consciousness. For example, we believe that we continue to exist while we sleep. What is it that continues to exist? If we say that the "body" continues to exist, what is meant by the "body"? The extended character of the visual field does not continue to exist, for by hypothesis our eyes are closed. It may be said that physical processes are going on while we sleep, and the system of these processes constitute the "body." But this is just the point. I wish to know the nature of these physical processes. To say that they consist in matter and motion merely pushes the inquiry back one step further, since what is meant by matter and motion? I know what the terms mean in terms of immediate experience; but I do not know what they refer to if they refer to something entirely divorced from experience. The notion of the existence of the "body" must be given meaning in terms of the occurrence of certain events, rhythms, and transactions, rather than in terms of matter. But what is meant by the term "event" or "rhythm" or "transaction"? We cannot now appeal to the common-sense notions of solidity and extension. Such terms have meaning only as elements in feeling.

We have seen, however, that the events which constitute our conscious life history are perceptions and feelings. We can mean, then, by the existence of the "body" or the existence of a sleeping person that

[1] And as Whitehead, Bradley, Clifford, Mach, and Leibniz have used it.

there exists a system of feelings or perceptions which are not conscious. Of course, in order to know about the existence of such feelings, we must consciously experience them, but feelings can exist without themselves being elements in other feelings. The ambiguity that creates the difficulty at this point lies in the term "know." When the phenomenalist or solipsist asks how we can know about the existence of the external world, his question is ambiguous. If he means that it is impossible to have certain knowledge about something not directly experienced, I should agree. But if he means that I cannot know what I mean by the existence of the "external world" what he says is false. I can give no meaning to the independent existence of extended substance, but I can give meaning to the independent existence of other feelings or experiences. The solipsist must give meaning to the notion of other experiences besides his present experience, otherwise he cannot give meaning to the complete sentence which states his view. The phenomenalist who admits the reality of the series of perceptions which constitutes his own life history has a cogent argument only against naive materialists.[1]

There are two things which metaphysics or a concern with concrete fact asks of the natural sciences. (1) That the abstractions used by the natural sciences be capable of being derived from actual experience; and (2) that the conclusions of science have meanings in terms of such experience. The two "scientific" dogmas which stand in the way of any understanding of freedom and causation are those which Russell has called the basic dogmas of materialism, namely, "the

[1] A fuller discussion of solipsism will be given lower down.

sole reality of matter" and the "reign of law." These dogmas contain implicitly the denial of the possibility of both efficient causation and freedom. Because they do is my reason for devoting so much space and argument to the examination of the notion of matter. The existence of matter implies the impossibility of efficient causation; and even when this dogma is given up, confusion between the notions of efficient causation and determinism makes it impossible to understand the nature of either causation or freedom. The definitions I have employed distinguish sharply between causation and determinism; and I believe that I have succeeded in establishing the historical significance of these definitions. Once it is realized that determinism is not implied by causation, that supposed antinomy of human reason, the problem of freedom may be seen as it is: a false antinomy engendered by a confusion. I cannot undertake to show specifically the manner in which our definitions solve most of the problems that have centered around the conception of human freedom, but I can choose two well-known problems.

There is, first, the common assertion that without a doctrine of necessity we can hold no one responsible for the consequences of his actions; and on the other hand the equally common reply that if the actions of a human being are necessitated we cannot hold him responsible for his actions. Thus Clarke held the latter view, whereas Hume held that "According to the hypothesis of liberty, therefore a man is as pure and untainted, after having committed the most horrid crimes. . . . It is only upon the principles of necessity that a person acquires any merit or demerit from his actions...."[1] It is clear that Clarke is right, and that if a man's actions are necessitated, he cannot be held morally responsible. But it is also clear that, unless a man actually *causes* future consequences, he cannot be held responsible for them. Hume fails to see that what is required is causal efficacy and not necessity. We do not hold a man absolutely responsible for everything that follows from his actions. We recognize the possibility of consequences over which the individual has no control. The affirmation of liberty is not the assertion of the absolute independence of events or actions, but the assertion that an event is causally efficacious or active in its own right. For this reason most of the seventeenth-century thinkers defined liberty or freedom not as indifference or independence but as "power." This is clearly the meaning Locke gave to freedom. Descartes provided for power or freedom at the price of a cleavage in his philosophic system. He did not place freedom in the indifference of the will but in its "power" to choose and assent. Even Malebranche defined liberty as a "power" of the soul and at the very moment when he denied it as a character of matter: "To understand this rightly, we must know, there's a very considerable difference between the impression of motion the Author of nature produces in Matter, and the impression of motion towards Good in general, wherewith the same Author of Nature continually influences our soul: For Matter is wholly inactive; it has no power of retarding, or stopping its motion, or determining and turning it one way rather than another.... But 'tis not so with the will, which may in one sense be said

[1] *Treatise*, II, 124.

to be active, and to have a *Power* in itself of giving a different determination to the inclination or impression it receives from God. . . . And by that *Liberty*, I mean nothing more than *the power* the mind has of turning that impression. . . ."[1] Here the identity of the notions of freedom and causation or power can plainly be seen. Yet Malebranche is traditionally regarded as the source of the notion that power or cause means necessary connection.[2] There is in this problem of responsibility, I think, no antinomy but only a confusion. Events or actions are causally related as they are related, but since no series of events necessitates any action, the individual may be held responsible for his actions. This is not to deny the influence of external factors. We can, on this view, excuse someone because we feel that the weight of influence was too great to be substantially modified. This only restates the view of common sense. We expect a man to exhibit the influences of his environment; but we do not regard it as a miracle if he does not. Similarly in the case of consequences, we realize that a man's actions are causally efficacious and that therefore he is responsible for his conduct; but we do not think that his actions necessitate any consequences and therefore we do not hold him absolutely responsible. Freedom and causal efficacy are essential in giving meaning to moral responsibility, but the doctrine of necessity is not.

Secondly, I wish to consider the Kantian antinomy of freedom. Kant recognized that freedom was a kind

---

[1] Malebranche, *Search After Truth*, 3. Italics mine.

[2] If Malebranche did mean by "power" necessary connection, he undoubtedly used the term in contradictory senses.

of causality, but he regarded it as opposed to "causality according to the laws of nature." In terms of the preceding discussion it is clear that the opposition which Kant is considering is not the opposition between causation and freedom but between determinism and freedom, that is to say, between determinism and causation. In discussing "causality according to the laws of nature" he says that ".... everything that takes place presupposes an anterior state on which it follows *inevitably* according to a rule."[1] There is here no description of the causal relation (taken as a matter-of-fact relation) nor is there any suggestion of efficiency or activity. There is instead the bold assertion of necessary connection or determinism. In discussing freedom, Kant introduces various terms which suggest efficiency or activity. He speaks of "effective causes," "spontaneity" and "production." His argument against these concepts lies in the claim that the admission of such relations between events destroys the unity of experience. This means only that the admission of such causes or "freedom" destroys any pretension we make to certain knowledge of matter of fact. There is here a genuine antinomy only if we assert that we possess certain knowledge (of things unexperienced), and that things are necessarily connected. In this case we could not admit the direct experience of activity and freedom. But the solution of this antinomy is obvious. The claim to certain knowledge is a vain pretension; and the truth of determinism is not a presupposition of ordered experience. Kant's third antinomy appears genuine because it seems to assert an opposition between causation and freedom;

[1] Immanuel Kant, *The Critique of Pure Reason*, 362. Italics mine.

but it is not genuine because it really asserts an opposition between determinism and causation (or freedom).

In Kant's time it was undoubtedly the case that the form of scientific laws implied the assertion that the events that constitute nature are determined. It is still widely believed that determinism, although it cannot be asserted as true, is a necessary presupposition of scientific method. Thus Hobson, who considers carefully the possibility of deterministic systems, declares: "The conclusion of the whole matter seems to be that the conception that the whole world of physical phenomena, or that a finite part of that world, is theoretically capable of being represented by a unified deterministic scheme is unproved and unprovable."[1] Yet Hobson believes that science uses and should use the concept of determinism as a working hypothesis. "But it is a working hypothesis employed in all the more advanced departments and stages of scientific thought, that tracts of phenomena can be discovered, to which deterministic schemes can be applied for the purposes of precise description and prediction."[2]

Never having engaged in actual scientific practice I know little of the requisites of scientific method. But Eddington declares that science is embarked on the formulation of a scheme of indeterministic laws,

---

[1] Hobson, *The Domain of Natural Science*, 98. We have seen that we cannot continue to sensibly assert an unproved and unprovable determinism because it is essential to the concept of determinism that it be capable of proof or demonstration.

[2] Idem. Hobson's conclusions that science does employ the concept of determinism and that it does not employ the concept of efficient causation show clearly that he distinguished the two concepts.

and that the hypothesis of determinism is no longer essential to scientific method. "The feature of the present situation is that, whether permanently or temporarily, determinism has disappeared altogether from the basis of modern physics. That is a statement of fact, not a prophecy, and so far as I am aware, there is no disagreement about the fact. The physicist may or may not believe in determinism, but in his own domain he has at present no evidence for it and, what is more, he has at present no use for it."[1] If we give up the assumption of determinism, it does not follow that attempts at precise description or prediction are discarded. One modern thinker has pointed out that the discarding of pretensions to theoretical predictability has led to increase in practical predictability. "Nevertheless . . . so far as predictability is concerned, the diminution in theoretical predictability has been attained by an increase in practical predictability in physics, since our physical knowledge has increased and therefore our powers of prediction."[2] It seems clear that the affirmation of the freedom of events does not entail an affirmation that the universe is chaotic or that scientific laws or prediction is impossible. In a previous chapter I have mentioned the different possible interpretations of the concept of "scientific law" or "law of nature." For my purposes it is necessary to point out only that the concept of "laws of nature" need not involve determinism. And I take the statement from Eddington, quoted above, as conclusive evidence of this fact.

[1] A. S. Eddington, *Indeterminacy and Indeterminism*, Aristotelian Society, Supplementary Volume x, 162.

[2] R. B. Braithwaite, *Indeterminacy and Indeterminism*, Aristotelian Society, Supplementary Volume x, 183.

The question of freedom is thus left entirely open so far as scientific laws are concerned.

Various scientists (Eddington, Weyl, Millikan, etc.) who were aware that the results of their special fields of inquiry had been used by philosophers of certain schools to disparage the evidence of direct experience, were among the first to point out that freedom is perfectly compatible with the results of scientific investigation and the formulation of these results in laws. But the philosophers of these schools, robbed of their scientific support, are careful to point out that the scientists are not to be trusted when they leave the field of exact investigation to venture opinions on philosophic questions. So be it. But if scientists are not to be trusted when they speak of philosophic matters, then we can dispense with the whole "mechanical mythology" and the initial denial of freedom. It is not sensible to disparage direct experience because of what "science says," and then to maintain that scientists are not to be trusted when they deny that what they say does disparage direct experience. Consider the case of someone immediately aware of his own freedom. He is told that if he knew more science, he would recognize that his experience of freedom is a delusion and that his actions are determined. Suppose this someone to study science and discover that science says nothing which could be significantly interpreted to mean that his experience of freedom is delusive. He is then told that as a student of science he is barred from saying anything significant about the question of freedom.

This example is a parody of Spinoza's assertion that freedom is an illusion born of ignorance. "It will be sufficient if I take here as an axiom that which no one ought to dispute, namely, that man is born ignorant of the causes of things, and that he has a desire of which he is conscious, to seek that which is profitable to him. From this it follows, firstly, that he thinks himself free because he is conscious of his wishes and appetites, whilst at the same time he is ignorant of the causes by which he is led to wish and desire. . . ."[1] In the first place, it is doubtful whether it is true, much less axiomatic, that we are born "conscious of desires"; if a man is born ignorant of the causes of his desires, he is also born ignorant of his desires. In the second place, we are conscious of external forces long before we attain self-consciousness or consciousness of our own desires. In the third place, a man might study the causes of his desires and discover such causes without it implying that he is not free. No amount of study could lead to the knowledge that his desires were necessitated or determined. Spinoza's argument here gains cogency because he substitutes the term "cause" with its common-sense implications for the term "necessary," which he should have used. He makes the opposition one between freedom and causation, when it should be between freedom or causation and determinism. When Spinoza denies freedom he does not mean only that there are discoverable connections between events. "That thing is called necessary, or rather compelled, which by another is determined to existence and action in a fixed and prescribed manner."[2] All things so determined are determined by God, so that no finite entity or action can be a cause. Spinoza's difficulty is that

[1] *Ethics*, Pt. I, App., 39. [2] Ibid., Def. VII, 2.

FREEDOM AND UNIFORMITY

he makes the dichotomy between freedom and causation too sharp. He gives us the alternative of regarding a thing as *causa sui* in the absolute sense or as determined in the absolute sense. It is clear that only God can be *causa sui* and that all finite things, since they are determined by God, must be absolutely determined. If we drop the reference to God we can understand how the question of events or entities being *causa sui* refers to a matter of degree. Any event inherits the causal influence which it does inherit; and it is *causa sui* or free to the degree that it is.

It is only because each event is free that we can regard each event as a cause. In terms of our initial definitions an event cannot be a cause unless it is free. And I do not think any meaning can be given to the notion of a causal agent that does not involve the freedom of such an agent. If we turn back to the difficulty which, as Eddington has pointed out, meets us when we try to render the notions of causation and determinism compatible, we can see clearly why this is so. Eddington's statement is as follows: "But curiously enough this elementary notion of cause and effect is quite inconsistent with a strictly causal scheme. How can I cause an event in the absolute future if the future was predetermined before I was born? The notion (of cause and effect) evidently implies that something may be born into the world at the instant Here-now, which has an influence extending throughout the future cone but no corresponding linkage to the cone of absolute past."[1] Eddington is here saying that the elementary notion of causal influence involves the notion of freedom. If any event

[1] Eddington, *The Nature of the Physical World*, 295.

is a genuine cause, exerts a genuine influence on the future, it is false to say that the future was determined before the occurrence of that event, so that the event itself is determined. If the event is a significant cause it is free—"Something is born into the world here and now"—which has an influence on the future and which is not derivable from the past. Even if in any given case an event transmits exactly the influence it received, the event must still be regarded as free. For the transmission is an act of the event itself. We cannot say an event is a cause unless it does something, exhibits power, in which case it is free. It is true that in cases where influence is transmitted without modification, we are not inclined to stress the freedom of the event, but only that it is a member of a series of causes.

II

The last topic which I shall consider is the question of the validity of induction and the concept of the uniformity of nature. I shall not attempt any final answers; but I shall indicate the direction in which I think the answers are to be found. If I can succeed in throwing light on these questions, the conclusions reached in the previous chapters, and the definitions which functioned as tools in reaching them, will receive their final justification. Russell, who surveys this problem in the concluding chapter of his *Analysis of Matter*, says: "We cannot escape from the solipsist position without bringing in induction and causality, which are still subject to the doubts arising from Hume's sceptical criticism."[1] The method by which

[1] Op. cit., 398.

we lay the sceptical doubts arising from Hume's criticism is, in outline, Whitehead's answer to Hume.[1] For Whitehead, the uniformity of nature is a consequence of the community of subjective form shared by the actual occasions constituting the environment of any given occasion. Exactly why this is an answer can be seen if we investigate the three terms used by Russell in his statement of the difficulty. In the first place solipsism means that only the present act of experience is real and that the existence of anything beyond the present act of experience cannot be reasonably asserted. This type of solipsism has been called by Santayana "solipsism of the present moment." It is the ultimate position to which transcendental criticism reduces solipsism. A solipsism which asserts the reality of the "I" as a ground of experience, loses under transcendental criticism its neat simplicity; it must either be taken as asserting a transcendental ego for which there is no experiential evidence or it must admit the reality of past and future experiences which constitute the life history of the "I". But since in this case there is the admission of the significant existence of something not directly given in a single intuition or experience, there is a tacit appeal to the validity of memory and causal influence. Thus Whitehead points out that Hume's appeal to memory and his use of the doctrine of force and liveliness involves an admission of the causal relation of occasions and hence of the community of subjective form constituting the settled world regarded as the environment of any given experience. But can Whitehead's view be regarded as a significant answer to Santayana's careful restriction

---

[1] *Process and Reality*, Chap. VIII, sect. v–viii, 303 et seq.

of solipsism to a "solipsism of the present moment"? I think that it can—for the nerve of Santayana's argument rests upon a failure to admit "ideas of reflection" and a tacit identification of sensuous perception with perception in general. Santayana, who is sceptical to the point of asserting that "nothing given exists," nevertheless tells us that we can have reasonable proof of the existence of intuitions: "The first existence, then, of which a sceptic who finds himself in the presence of random essences may gather reasonable proof, is the existence of the intuition to which those essences are manifest. This is of course not the object which the animal mind first posits and believes in. The existence of things is assumed by animals in action and expectation before intuition supplies any description of what the thing is that confronts them in a certain quarter. But animals are not sceptics, and a long experience must intervene before the problem arises which I am here considering, namely, whether anything need be posited and believed in at all. And I reply that it is not inevitable, if I am willing and able to look passively on the essences that may happen to be given: but if I consider what they are, and how they appear, I see that this appearance is an accident to them; that the principle of it is a contribution from my side, which I call intuition. The difference between essence and intuition, though men may have discovered it late, then seems to me profound and certain."[1] Santayana may rest his belief in a "material world" on sheer animal faith, and thus avoid any necessity of justifying such a belief. But the existence of intuition is not a matter of faith; it is

[1] G. Santayana, *Scepticism and Animal Faith*, 133.

"profound and certain." Now the possibility of being certain of the existence of an intuition rests upon the fact that an intuition must be intuited; that is to say, we must recognize that in "ideas of reflection" we have immediate experience of our own intuitions, actions or perceptions. Of course no perception perceives itself. Any act of perception can only be a datum or an object for a subsequent act of perception. This is why those philosophers who restricted their analysis of experience to *one* act of experience have reported that they found only the objects of experience and no act of experiencing. If we analyse any specific experience we cannot find the *act* of experience contained as a content within itself. But the mere fact that the analysis of experience or intuitions is possible is evidence that we not only experience essences but that we experience intuitions. Otherwise how is it possible to distinguish between essence and intuition? The cases in which there is a direct and obvious intuition of intuitions or experience of experiences are cases similar to those discussed as evidence of a direct perception of causal influence. Whitehead calls physical causation "blind memory." Conscious memory is consciousness of causal efficacy. By "memory" here I do not mean the recollection of events in the distant past; "memory" refers to the perception of the immediate past. Because of the practical significance of sensuous perception for future action, this reference to the past is reduced to a minimum. This is the point of Bergson's attack on sensation as a source of theoretical knowledge. We confuse practical importance with theoretical importance. An animal is more interested in the future experiences he can infer from visual sense data than he is in introspectively observing the causal development of his intuitions. But the fallacy of "spatialization" is not an inherent disorder of the human mind. So long as it appeared that even the most advanced of sciences were guilty of this fallacy, Bergson was justified in regarding it as an innate weakness of the mind; but now that modern science has caught up with Berkeley, it seems clear that the fallacy has its source in a confusion of "essence" and "existence," of the "abstract" and the "concrete." The genuine significance of Santayana's discussion lies in the fact that he recognizes that intuitions or perceptions exist and that the objects of any intuition *qua* objects, do not exist.

Thus our answer to solipsism rests upon a factual assertion, namely, that there is direct experience of past experiences. The same assertion gives meaning to the concept of causation. We perceive causal influences when we perceive "force and liveliness" transmitted from one occasion of experience to another.

The final question is how, in terms of this account, the notion of "induction" can be rescued from Hume's sceptical doubts. Stated simply the problem is one of giving a reasonable justification for the belief in the uniformity of nature or the belief that the future will resemble the past. Hume states that the principle of this belief must be that "instances of which we have had no experience must resemble those of which we have had experience, and that the course of nature continues always uniformly the same."[1] This principle cannot be demonstrated because it is not inconceivable that the course of nature will change. But neither,

[1] *Treatise*, I, 89.

Hume thinks, can the principle be justified in terms of experience, since it questions the possibility of significant knowledge concerning those objects and relations not experienced. It has been pointed out by Laird and others[1] that the force of Hume's argument rests upon the supposition of empty time. Hume supposes a succession of empty future moments and asks how we can know anything about the contents of these moments. It seems clear, however, that when we ask questions about the future we can ask about the nature of an entity in a specified environment or about the nature of the environment of a certain specified entity. We cannot have even probable knowledge about an unknown entity in an unknown environment. When Hume asks how we can know anything about the future, he tacitly presupposes that some entity capable of knowledge will exist in the future. He supposes that this entity will have a body and a mind and certain sorts of experiences. Now the doctrine of the inheritance of subjective form implies that any actual entity will exhibit the influences of the entities which constitute its environment. Hence the future existence of experiences analogous to present experiences, presupposes the future existence of an environment analogous to the present environment. On the other hand, the future existence of an analogous environment provides for the future existence of analogous experiences. Hume's question is unanswerable if it implies an unspecified entity in an unspecified environment; but such questions need not be answered. Without the assumption of the future existence of entities capable of perceiving, thinking, and feeling,

[1] J. Laird, *Hume's Philosophy of Human Nature*, 108-9.

questions about the future processes of nature are non-significant. But if we assume the future existence of such entities we already have assumed something concerning the nature of the environment.

Judgments of probability are made on the basis of evidence present to the judging individual. This evidence in its immediate non-statistical form is the vague intuition of the general causal influence of the environment, including the past occasions of the individual's history. If I expect to eat breakfast to-morrow, I am presupposing the general continuance of the type of environment and the type of events which usually ensue in my eating breakfast. On the other hand, if I expect that the sun will rise to-morrow and that the oxygen content of the atmosphere will not suffer a drastic diminution, I am presupposing that I shall be alive, breathing, perceiving light, and no doubt eating breakfast. "Another way of stating this explanation of the validity of induction is, that in every forecast there is a presupposition of a certain type of actual entities, and that the question then asked is, Under what circumstances will these entities find themselves? The reason that an answer can be given is that the presupposed type of entities requires a presupposed type of data for the primary phases of these actual entities; and that a presupposed type of data requires a presupposed type of social environment. But the laws of nature are the outcome of the social environment. Hence, when we have presupposed a type of actual occasions, we have already some information as to the laws of nature in operation throughout the environment. . . . It is at this point that the organic philosophy differs from any form of Cartesian 'substance-philosophy.' For if a substance requires nothing but itself in order to exist, its survival can tell no tale as to the survival of order in its environment."[1]

Hume's sceptical doubts are undoubtedly Cartesian in origin. "In short there are two principles which I cannot render consistent, nor is it in my power to renounce either of them, viz. *that all our distinct perceptions are distinct existences, and that the mind never perceives any real connection among distinct existences.*"[2] If by "real connection" Hume means necessary connection, the second principle is self-evident; but if he means a matter-of-fact causal connection, it is empirically false.

Whether or not the falsity of this principle robs Hume's attack on the validity of induction of its merits, is a question which I do not intend to answer here. I think, however, that in view of the emphasis which Hume placed on this principle, and in view of its falsity, the whole question of induction requires re-examination on grounds other than Hume's. Whitehead has attempted such a re-examination, an outline of which I have given above. I believe that a satisfactory answer lies in the direction of such considerations (whether or not my brief exposition is itself satisfactory).

The belief in the uniformity of nature arises from the recognition of the differing degrees in which any single event is dominated by its environment. The settled conditions of the world are those general characters exhibited by the systematic interconnection

---

[1] *Process and Reality*, 311.
[2] *Treatise*, Appendix, 319; Italics Hume's.

of the entities which constitute the world. The immense number of these events as contrasted with the free activity of any individual event, makes such free activity practically unimportant so far as the general order of nature is concerned. But the recognition by modern scientists that order is statistical (and not imposed by God) illustrates the fact that this free activity cannot be entirely disregarded. The closer science comes to the consideration of the behaviour of individual events, the further it departs from statements of uniformity. Acts of perception, or will, or desire, are individual events. They exhibit the influence of the past. But when we consider them directly we are sensible not so much of the grand uniformities of nature but of the free activity of each individual event.

APPENDIX

ON THE REALISM OF G. E. MOORE

IF, as Moore argues,[1] the nerve of the idealistic argument consists in the *esse est percipi*, Moore's paper must be considered as a final and complete refutation of idealism. But Berkeley asserts that *esse is percipi only when applied to sensible things*. "And (to me) it seems no less evident that the various sensations or ideas imprinted on the sense, however blended or combined together (that is, whatever objects they compose) cannot exist otherwise than in a mind perceiving them. I think an intuitive knowledge may be obtained of this by anyone that shall attend to *what is meant by the term exist*, when applied to sensible things ... Their *esse* is *percipi* ..."[2] In another article[3] Moore recognizes that Berkeley restricts the *esse est percipi* to sense qualities for he says: "Now, with one class of these philosophers—the class to which I think Berkeley belongs—I think I can put myself right comparatively easily. The philosophers I mean are those who say that it is only in the case of one particular class of contents (the kind of 'content' which Berkeley calls 'ideas'), that is to say, 'the content A exists' is to say 'A is perceived,' and who admit that in the case of other contents—myself and my perceptions and thought, for example—to say that these exist or are real, is to say of them something

---

[1] *Philosophical Studies*, "Refutation of Idealism."

[2] Berkeley, *Principles of Human Knowledge*, 114; italics Berkeley's.

[3] *Philosophical Studies*, "The Nature and Reality of Objects of Perception," 73.

different from this. These philosophers admit, that is to say, that the word 'exists' has two different senses and that in only one of these senses is it synonymous with the words 'is perceived.'" Moore goes on to ask if a common meaning can be found for these two usages of the term "exists." He is sure that the being or the existence of perceptions does not consist in being perceived, so that the meaning of the term "exist" cannot be "is perceived." However, he reaches no answer in his search for a common meaning. "But it may be asked: What is this common simple sense of the word exists? For my own part it seems to me so simple that it cannot be expressed in other words except those which are recognized as its synonyms. I think we are all perfectly familiar with its meaning: it is the meaning which you understood me to have throughout this paper until I began this discussion."[1] Contrary to Moore's consoling conclusion I do not believe that "we are all perfectly familiar with the meaning of 'exists.'" Rather I hold with Berkeley that the "vulgar opinion involves a contradiction." Throughout Moore's paper I was not aware of understanding the meaning of the term as he used it; and I had hoped at the beginning of the explicit discussion that he would reach some definite conclusion.

In a similar difficulty, Plato, while looking for a meaning for existence which shall include both the

---

[1] *Philosophical Studies*, "The Nature and Reality of Objects of Perception," 78. In his search for the meaning of "exists" Moore does not consider the possibility of a definition in terms of space-time location; and he shows also that the definition of existence in terms of "systematic connection" with other things is "vitiated" by being "circular": "But when we look into their meaning, we find that what they mean is (what indeed is alone plausible)—systematically connected with other *real* things." Ibid., 77.

corporeal and the incorporeal, offers the following definition of existence: "I suggest that everything which possesses any power of any kind, whether to produce a change in anything of any nature or to be affected even in the least degree by the slightest cause, though it be only on one occasion, has real existence. For I set up as a definition which defines being, that it is nothing else than power."[1] It is obvious that, in terms of this definition, "matter" as defined by the seventeenth-century philosophers does not exist. And Berkeley makes use of this notion to show that a causal theory of perception which regards matter as a cause is self-contradictory. Further, Berkeley held, and more recently Santayana has argued, that objects of perception are devoid of power; they are lifeless essences—qualities without "life and motion."[2]

In so far as we use the term "exist" to refer to perceptions, we are using it in accordance with Plato's definition. The objects of perception, however, being essences, do not exist in this sense. Yet the contents of perception are not nothing; they are just the characters that they are. The point is to discover whether any meaning can be given to the existence of any content out of relation to some perception. It is not a question of giving meaning to the existence of something unperceived. We have already done this

---

[1] *Sophist*, 247 E.

[2] It is for this reason that Plato refuses to take the Socratic "doctrine of ideas" as a sufficient statement of the meaning of the "real": "But for heaven's sake, shall we let ourselves easily be persuaded that motion and life and soul and mind are really not present to absolute being, that it neither lives nor thinks, but awful and holy, devoid of mind, is fixed and immovable?" *Sophist*, 249 A.

when we assert the existence of acts of perception. The question now concerns only the unperceived existence of "objects" of perception. Moore recognizes that this question is in some sense linked up with the question of abstraction. "For there is a certain doctrine, very prevalent among philosophers nowadays, which by a very simple reduction may be seen to assert that two distinct things (perception and object) both are and are not distinct. A distinction is asserted; but it is also asserted that the things distinguished form an 'organic unity.' But forming such a unity it is held, each would not be what it is apart from its relation to the other. Hence to consider either by itself is to make an illegitimate abstraction. The recognition that there are organic unities and illegitimate abstractions in this sense is regarded as one of the chief conquests of modern philosophy. But what is the sense attached to these terms? An abstraction is illegitimate, when and only when we attempt to assert of a part—of something abstracted—that which is true only of the whole to which it belongs: and it may perhaps be useful to point out that this should not be done."[1] The note on which this passage ends seems to indicate that Moore thinks that no one has ever been guilty of such illegitimate abstraction. But is not the assertion of the existence of sense-qualities an illegitimate abstraction of just the kind which Moore thinks erroneous? Existence applies to the whole, to the act of perception. What exists is the "perception of A" or the "subject-object" complex. To assert of a part, of something abstracted—that is to say, of the object—that it exists, is to be guilty of

[1] *Philosophical Studies*, "Refutation of Idealism," 14–15.

illegitimate abstraction, of what Whitehead has called the "fallacy of misplaced concretion." The only sense in which sense-qualities can legitimately be said to exist is the sense in which they are perceived, that is to say, as parts of a whole which exists. We may consider sense qualities in divorce from the act of perceiving; this is properly called abstraction. However, the abstraction becomes illegitimate when we ascribe to the abstraction we are considering a character which pertains to the whole from which the object of our consideration was abstracted.

Berkeley was aware that the error contained in the assertion of the independent existence of sensible things had its root in an erroneous abstraction. "V. Cause of this prevalent error.—If we thoroughly examine this tenet, it will perhaps, be found at bottom to depend on the doctrine of abstract ideas. For can there be a nicer strain of abstraction than to distinguish the existence of sensible objects from their being perceived so as to conceive them *existing* unperceived?"[1] Berkeley does not protest against considering the sensible quality in divorce from the perception; but he does object to the attempt to consider the sensible qualities as *existing* in divorce from perception.

Berkeley's arguments have not been universally accepted because his positive conclusions are unwarranted. He shows that what exists are always acts of perception, or perceptions; but he concludes to the existence of "spiritual substance." If we understand by spiritual substance merely sentient or perceiving substance, there is no difficulty here. But Berkeley's use of the term "spiritual substance" gives a religious

[1] Berkeley, *A New Theory of Vision, and Other Writings*, 115.

and rationalistic significance to his conclusions. He does not of course prove the existence of spirits in the sense of immortal souls; nor does he show that every substance must be conscious. But he has made it clear that what exists outside of or independently of any perception must be another perception; and that there is not the slightest reason for assuming the existence of non-sentient or extended substance.

I have used the term "sentient" because it is in feeling that we can secure an ostensive definition of "power." But if the term is disliked because it suggests consciousness, Plato's term "power" may be substituted. The important point is that we cannot argue from the "passivity" of sense-qualities to the conclusion that what exists is incapable of entering into causal relations.

BIBLIOGRAPHY

Aristotelian Society: Supplementary Volume X, "Indeterminism, Formalism and Value," Harrison and Sons, Ltd., London, 1931.

Berkeley, George, *A New Theory of Vision and Other Writings*, Everyman's Library, 1910.

Broad, C. D., *Perception, Physics, and Reality*, Cambridge, The University Press, 1914.

Church, R., *Hume's Theory of the Understanding*, London, G. Allen and Unwin Ltd., 1935.

Church, R., *A Study in the Philosophy of Malebranche*, London, G. Allen and Unwin Ltd., 1931.

Descartes, R., *Philosophical Works*, translated by E. L. Haldane and G. R. T. Ross, vols. i and ii, Cambridge, The University Press, 1911.

Eddington, A. S., *Space, Time and Gravitation*, Cambridge, The University Press, 1920.

Eddington, A. S., *The Nature of the Physical World*, Cambridge, The University Press; New York, The Macmillan Company, 1929.

Galilei, Galileo, *Dialogues Concerning the Two Great Systems of the World*, translated by Thomas Salusbury, and included in his *Mathematical Collections and Translations*, vol. i, London, 1661.

Galilei, Galileo, *Two New Sciences*, translated from the Italian and Latin into English by Henry Crew and Alfonso De Salvio, New York, The Macmillan Company, 1914.

Gibson, J., *Locke's Theory of Knowledge and its Historical Relations*, Cambridge, The University Press, 1917.

Gilbert, William, *On the Loadstone and Magnetic Bodies* (Mottelay translation), New York, 1893.

Hobbes, Thomas, *The English Works of Thomas Hobbes of Malmesbury*, edited by Sir William Molesworth, London, 1845.

Hobson, E. W., *The Domain of Natural Science*, New York, The Macmillan Company, 1923.

Hume, David, *Inquiry Concerning Human Understanding; and an Inquiry Concerning the Principles of Morals*, edited by L. A. Selby-Bigge, second edition, Oxford, The Clarendon Press, 1902.

Hume, David, *A Treatise of Human Nature*, Everyman's Library, 1911.

Kant, Immanuel, *Critique of Pure Reason*, translated by F. Max Müller, second edition, revised, New York, The Macmillan Company, 1927.

Keeling, S. V., *Descartes*, London, Ernest Benn, Ltd., 1934.

Laird, J., *Hume's Philosophy of Human Nature*, London, Methuen and Company, Ltd., 1932.

Lange, F.A., *The History of Materialism*, translated by E. C. Thomas, New York, Harcourt Brace and Company, Inc., 1925.

Leibniz, G. W. von, *Correspondence with Clarke*, printed for J. Knapton, London, 1717.

Leibniz, G. W. von, *Discourse on Metaphysics, Correspondence with Arnauld, etc.*, translated by Dr. G. R. Montgomery, Chicago, The Open Court Publishing Company, 1931.

Leibniz, G. W. von, *The Monadology and Other Philosophical Writings*, translated by Robert Latta, Oxford, The University Press, second impression, 1925.

Leibniz, G. W. von, *New Essays on Human Understanding*, translated by A. G. Langley, New York, The Macmillan Company, 1896.

Mach, Ernst, *The Science of Mechanics*, translated by T. J. McCormack, Chicago, The Open Court Publishing Company, 1902.

Malebranche, F., *Dialogues on Metaphysics and Religion*, translated by Morris Ginsberg, London, G. Allen and Unwin Ltd., 1913.

Malebranche, F., *Search after Truth*, translated by T. Taylor, London, 1700.

Moore, G. E., *Philosophical Studies*, New York, Harcourt Brace and Company, 1922.

Newton, I., *Mathematical Principles of Natural Philosophy*, translated into English by Andrew Motte; revised by Florian Cajori, University of California Press, Berkeley, 1934.

Plato, *Theaetetus and Sophist*, translated by H. N. Fowler, Loeb Classical Library, London, William Heinemann, Ltd., 1928.

Price, H. H., *Perception*, London, Methuen and Co., Ltd., 1932.

Russell, B. A. W., *The Analysis of Matter*, London, Routledge and Company; New York, Harcourt Brace and Company, 1927.

Russell, B. A. W., *A Critical Exposition of the Philosophy of Leibniz*, Cambridge, The University Press, 1900.

Santayana, G., *Scepticism and Animal Faith*, New York, Scribner's, 1923.

Smith, N. K., *Studies in Cartesian Philosophy*, New York, The Macmillan Company, 1902.

Spinoza, B. de, *Correspondence*, translated and edited by A. Wolf, London, G. Allen and Unwin, Ltd., 1928.

Spinoza, B. de, *Ethic*, translated from the Latin by W. Hale White; translation revised by Amelia Hutchison Stirling, fourth edition, Oxford, The University Press, 1930.

Taylor, H. O., *Thought and Expression in the Sixteenth Century*, New York, The Macmillan Company, 1920.

Weyl, H., *The Open World*, New Haven, The Yale University Press, 1932.

Whitehead, A. N., *Adventures of Ideas*, Cambridge, The University Press; New York, The Macmillan Company, 1933.

Whitehead, A. N., *Process and Reality*, Cambridge, The University Press; New York, The Macmillan Company, 1930.

Windelband, W., *A History of Philosophy*, translated by James H. Tufts, New York, The Macmillan Company, 1926.

Wisdom, John, *Problems of Mind and Matter*, Cambridge, The University Press, 1934.

Wolfson, H. A., *The Philosophy of Spinoza*, Cambridge, Mass., The Harvard University Press, 1934.

Zeller, E., *Outlines of the History of Greek Philosophy*, 13th edition, revised by Dr. Wilhelm Nestle and translated by L. R. Palmer, New York, Harcourt Brace and Company, 1931.

INDEX

Abstraction: 180
Action at a distance: 118
Agents and acts: 26–7
Arnauld: 121

Bacon: 105, 161, 209
Belief, causes of: 147–9
Belief in necessary connection: 146–7, 152–4
Bergson: 219, 245
Berkeley: 189, 215–19, 251–5
Bradley, F. H.: 181, 231 n.
Braithwaite: 197
Bramhall, Bishop of Derry: 50–9, 67, 90
Broad: 176–9, 183, 196 n.
Bruno: 209

Campanella: 209
Cartesians: 102 n., 118, 161–2
Causal influence, inconceivability of: 96
Causal theory of perception: 215–17
Causation, experience of, illusory: 36
Causation and determinism, opposition between: 108–9
Cause defined: 17–18
Causes, entities that can be: 25–6
Church: 21 n., 80, 81, 82, 85–6, 87 n., 102 n., 121 n.
Clarke: 29 n., 120 n., 233–4
Clifford: 228 n.
Cordemoy: 102 n.

Deductive knowledge: 210
Descartes: 17, 31, 36, 37, 38, 40, 41–9, 52, 60, 66 n., 68, 70, 96, 106, 123, 135, 161, 165, 174–5, 176, 188, 199, 200, 209, 210, 212–13, 216, 234
Descartes' theory of matter: 201–5
Determination of the mind: 147–9

Determinism, definition of: 32
Deterministic systems: 118–21

Eddington: 108, 120, 171, 184, 186–7, 228 n., 237, 239, 241
External world: 178–79, 183

Feeling: 228, 230–2
Final cause: 161
Free, entities that can be: 29
Freedom, definition of: 28
Freedom, indubitability of: 37
Freedom of the will: 30–3

Galileo: 40, 113–15, 161
Gassendi: 43, 162
Gibson: 17, 20
Gilbert: 209
God as the cause of essence: 69–70
God as the cause of existence: 69–70
God, meaning of, for Spinoza: 60–3
Gravity: 116–17

Hobbes: 20 n., 41, 50–9, 70, 90, 91, 105, 112, 161, 173–4, 180 n., 213, 218
Hobson: 227, 237
Hume: 7, 13, 19, 20, 21, 27, 36, 79, 81–2, 102, 109–13, 124–5, 127–9, 130–54, 158–60, 175–6, 178, 189–90, 197–8, 200, 207 n., 233–4, 243, 246–9
Hume's confusion of power and necessity: 25

Immanent cause, God as: 122
Induction: 242–50

Kant: 7, 126, 154, 235–7
Kepler: 161

La Forge: 102 n.
Laird: 21 n., 141 n.
Lamettrie: 212
Lange: 212
Laplace: 106–8, 192
Law of Causation: 7–9
Laws of motion: 166–7, 170–2, 193, 206
Laws of nature: 104–5, 238
Leibniz: 13, 14, 17, 18, 19, 20, 26, 27, 28, 29 n., 40, 41, 49, 87–100, 123, 135, 155, 161, 163–6, 172, 176, 177, 178, 180 n., 182–3, 184, 188, 190, 209, 212, 219, 228
Leonardo da Vinci: 209
Locke: 13, 14, 17, 18, 19, 20, 21, 26, 27, 29, 42, 141, 155, 159–60, 165, 166, 167–8, 176, 178, 205, 213–15, 216, 234
Lotze: 177
Lucretius: 208

Mach: 105–6, 227
McTaggart: 177
Malebranche: 14, 21, 22–4, 41, 45, 75–87, 102 n., 111–12, 123, 135, 168–9, 176, 234–5
Materialism: 192
Matter, reality of: 208–21
Millikan: 239
Moore: 213, 217, 229, 251–5

Natura naturans and *natura naturata*: 62–3
Necessary connection: 19, 23, 33
Necessitation, extrinsic: 50–1
Necessitation, hypothetical: 50–1, 57–8, 88–90
Necessity of supposition or definition: 67
Newton: 42, 115–18, 166–7, 176, 209
Newtonians: 161–2

Occasional causes: 48
Occasional and real causes, distinction between: 79–80
Occasionalism: 35, 44
Occult causes: 161–3, 209–10
Oldenburg: 31

Pantheism in Spinoza: 65, 65 n.
Plato: 100 n., 252–3, 256
Power, source of the idea of: 21–2, 163–75
Pre-established harmony: 35 n., 165
Pure possibles: 88

Regularity view of causation: 122–4, 126–9
Russell: 184, 192, 196, 199–200, 207, 225–6, 232, 242–3

Santayana: 243–4
Science and theology: 103–6
Smith, N. K.: 45
Solidity: 205–6
Solipsism: 243–6
Spinoza: 15, 20 n., 30–2, 33, 36, 41, 59–75, 86, 161, 169–73, 176, 181, 221, 239–40
Substance, idea of: 190–1
Substantial forms: 98–9
Succession, analysis of: 179–82

Time, independence of moments of: 42

Uniformity and freedom: 131–4

Weyl: 239
Whitehead: 10, 156–8, 159, 160, 176, 220, 227, 243–9, 255
Windleband: 65, 103, 104, 105, 161
Wisdom, J.: 9 n.
Wolfson: 66 n.

For Product Safety Concerns and Information please contact our EU
representative GPSR@taylorandfrancis.com
Taylor & Francis Verlag GmbH, Kaufingerstraße 24, 80331 München, Germany

www.ingramcontent.com/pod-product-compliance
Lightning Source LLC
Chambersburg PA
CBHW071818300426
44116CB00009B/1356